Montana

Montana

Charles George and Linda George

Children's Press®
A Division of Grolier Publishing
New York   London   Hong Kong   Sydney
Danbury, Connecticut

Frontispiece: Sunset in Glacier National Park

Front cover: Big Hole Battlefield National Monument

Back cover: Long Lake in winter

Consultant: Brian Shovers, Reference Historian, Montana Historical Society

Please note: All statistics are as up-to-date as possible at the time of publication.

Visit Children's Press on the Internet at http://publishing.grolier.com

Book production by Editorial Directions, Inc.

Library of Congress Cataloging-in-Publication Data

George, Charles, 1949–
Montana / Charles George and Linda George.
  p. cm.—(America the beautiful. Second series)
Includes bibliographical references (p.) and index.
Summary: Describes the geography, plants and animals, history, economy, language,
  religions, culture, and people of the state of Montana.
ISBN 0-516-21092-0
  1. Montana—Juvenile literature. [1. Montana.] I. George, Linda. II. Title. III. Series.
F731.3.G46 2000
978.6—dc21   99-053521
                                                                              CIP
                                                                              AC

Acknowledgments

We wish to thank the office of Montana governor Marc Racicot for its help in researching this book. Many thanks also to Lucille Davis for her invaluable assistance in obtaining research materials. Finally, we would like to express our gratitude to the friendly people of Montana, especially those we met on our short trek over Beartooth Pass, into Billings, and through the southeastern corner of the state.

Red cliffs of the Terry
Badlands

Beartooth Mountains

Bighorn Canyon National
Recreation Area

Contents

Bitterroot

National Bison Range

Hiking in Glacier National Park

Anaconda

Sitting Bull

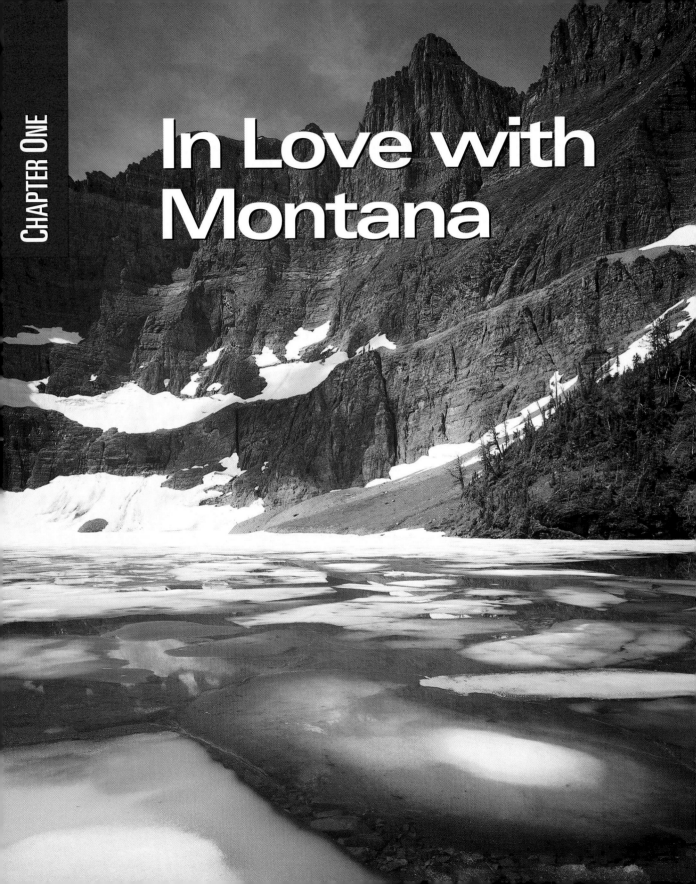

CHAPTER ONE

In Love with Montana

John Steinbeck said, "I am in love with Montana. For other states I have admiration, respect, recognition, even some affection, but with Montana it is love." Citizens of Montana agree wholeheartedly.

Many people are drawn to the great outdoors of Montana.

From the vast, open spaces of the eastern part of the state to the forested mountains of the western part of the state, much of the terrain is still as Lewis and Clark found it almost two centuries ago. Only 5 persons per square mile (2 per square kilometer) live in Montana, and they are content to keep the state sparsely populated.

With more than forty state parks and hundreds of campgrounds, Montana attracts millions of visitors each year. They seek expansive landscapes, towering forests, some of the country's best hunting and fishing, or breathtaking views. All of these are to be found in the state named for its mountains.

Opposite: Iceberg Lake in the Rocky Mountains

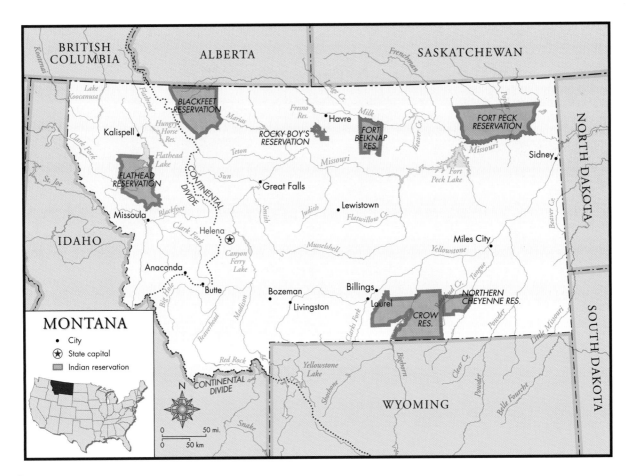

Geopolitical map of Montana

Rudyard Kipling, one of the British Empire's most beloved authors, once traveled to Montana by train and recorded his impressions in letters later published in a collection called *Sea to Sea: Letters of Travel* (1899). Stopping along the Yellowstone River east of Livingstone, Kipling enjoyed the hospitality and tall tales of a local character who called himself Yankee Jim. According to Kipling, Jim was "a picturesque old man with a talent for yarns." He "had known the Yellowstone country for years, and bore upon his body marks of Indian arrows."

Kipling followed Yankee Jim's recommendation to go to a stream that was "alive with trout." He later wrote, "At the fortieth trout I gave up counting; and I had reached the fortieth in less than two hours. They were small fish—not one over 2 pounds—but they fought like small tigers. . . . That was fishing, though [the hot sun] peeled the skin from my nose in strips."

So it has been for decades, and so it will continue for decades to come. Montana will forever inspire writers, poets, artists, historians, and visitors with its unique ambiance, exquisite beauty, and enough room to swing your arms in a circle without worrying about hitting anyone or anything. Take a deep breath of clean air, and experience Montana.

CHAPTER TWO

The Last Wilderness

Montana was one of the last states to be settled by both Native American tribes and white settlers. Written records began in the mid-1700s, but people have inhabited the area much longer.

Paleo-Indians, ancestors of modern Native Americans, first migrated to North America at least 10,000 years ago. These wanderers crossed a strip of land between Asia and North America across the Bering Sea. An ice age had caused ocean levels to drop, exposing this "land bridge."

Native Americans hunted buffalo in early Montana.

Descendants of these first immigrants made their way south from Alaska along the Great North Trail. Projectile points and primitive tools have been found near Alder, Montana City, Whitehall, and Lindsay. These Paleo-Indians lived mainly on the Plains and hunted woolly mammoths and prehistoric bison.

About 5,000 B.C., weather conditions changed the Great Plains into a desert, forcing hunters to move on. A different group, mostly gatherers from the desert southwest, then visited the western valleys.

The last group of Paleo-Indians arrived from the south and west 2,000 to 3,000 years ago. These hunters followed herds of bison to the area as more moderate weather developed. Tepee rings—circles

Opposite: Bighorn Canyon National Recreation Area

An Indian woman
treating a buffalo hide

of rocks used to secure the outer edges of a tepee—have been found in central and eastern Montana. These last arrivals were probably ancestors of the Flathead Indians.

Before they had horses and rifles, Native Americans used bows and arrows to hunt buffalo. They stampeded large herds over steep cliffs called *pishkuns* and harvested the dead animals. Sites of these "buffalo jumps" are found in central and eastern Montana.

Other evidence of early Montanans exists on cave walls and cliffs throughout the state. Pictographs, or rock paintings, and petroglyphs, or rock carvings, were made during this period.

Later Arrivals

The first Native Americans to arrive in Montana were probably the Shoshone, who came from the Great Basin in about 1600. The Crow arrived soon afterward, followed by the Blackfeet, or Siksika, in about 1730. Along with the Blackfeet came the Gros Ventre (also known as the Atsina) and the Assiniboine. They migrated west from the Great Lakes and the Mississippi Basin. The Dakota (known as Sioux), the Northern Cheyenne, the Chippewa, and the Cree arrived in the 1800s. White settlers in the Canadian prairies had forced these Indians southward.

Montana's Plains tribes—the Blackfeet, the Assiniboine, the Crow, the Cheyenne, and the Gros Ventre—lived in the grasslands and rolling hills of eastern Montana. Montana's plateau and mountain tribes—the Pend d'Oreille (also known as the Kalispel), the Kutenai, the Bannock, the Shoshone, and the Flathead (or Salish)—lived in the western mountains.

The Plains Tribes

In the early 1700s, almost 200 years after being brought to the Americas by Spanish explorers, horses were introduced to the Plains. They changed almost every aspect of life for the Plains tribes. Hunting became more efficient, groups moved more quickly into new territories, and earth lodges were abandoned for the easily transported skin-covered tepees.

Buffalo were especially important to the Plains Indians. Buffalo hides provided tepees and moccasins. Buffalo meat provided fresh food during hunting season and dried food during winter. The Plains tribes used bones as sewing needles, dried sinew as thread, manure as fuel for campfires, and buffalo tails as flyswatters.

The Mountain Tribes

Like the Plains Indians, Montana's plateau and mountain tribes were hunter-gatherers. They ate mostly deer, fish, roots, and berries. Accomplished horsemen, they frequently crossed the Rocky Mountains to hunt buffalo in the eastern foothills. The Shoshone were fearsome warriors and probably the first tribe to ride horses.

Many traditions of the mountain tribes, particularly the Flathead and the Kutenai, are associated with Pacific Northwest tribes.

Their homes, unlike the skin-covered tepees of Plains Indians, were more permanent lodges covered with bark or pine boughs.

Because of Pacific Coast cultural ties, some tribes in the northern Rocky Mountains held potlatches—great feasts during which the host gave away many of his possessions. Another common practice among mountain and plateau tribes was basket weaving. These people wove fine containers out of grasses, vines, or pine needles often to collect and store food.

Fierce conflicts sometimes arose over hunting territories. Smaller tribes such as the Flathead and the Kutenai also faced the wrath of the Blackfeet when they went hunting outside their mountain hideaways.

Blackfeet Indians setting fire to a Crow buffalo range

Early Exploration and Trapping

Montana was originally part of France's claim in the Americas. In 1682, French explorers along the Gulf Coast claimed Louisiana as French land.

In 1743, the French brothers François and Louis Joseph de La Vérendrye are thought to have entered the southeastern corner of the state from the Dakotas, looking for furs for their father's company. They reported "shining mountains" in the distance, probably the Bighorn Mountains.

Other French and Spanish trappers and traders followed, trading for furs with local tribes and sometimes taking Native American wives. In 1762, the lands were ceded to Spain, who returned them to France in the Treaty of San Ildefonso in 1800.

Explorers Meriwether Lewis and William Clark

The Lewis and Clark Expedition

In 1803, France sold the territory to the United States. The Louisiana Purchase, which almost doubled the land area of the United States, included most of what is today Montana.

In 1804, President Thomas Jefferson sent two men—Meriwether Lewis, his private secretary and longtime friend, and William Clark—to explore and map the region.

Departing from St. Louis, Missouri, on May 14, 1804, Lewis and Clark's expedition, with some forty soldiers, guides, and interpreters, moved slowly up the Missouri River. They spent the winter in a North Dakota Mandan village. The following spring, with new guides and interpreters—Toussaint Charbonneau and his Shoshone wife, Sacajawea—the expedition continued upriver in canoes and keelboats.

Crossing into the region that is now Montana on April 26, 1805, Lewis and Clark followed the Missouri to its headwaters near the Continental Divide. Along the way, they recorded their observations in journals, charting the location of mountains, waterfalls, and rivers. They also described and sketched local plants, animals, and Native Americans.

When Lewis and Clark reached the snowy barrier of the Continental Divide, Sacajawea's people—the Shoshone—helped the expedition cross the Rocky Mountains. The explorers followed the Clearwater, Snake, and Columbia Rivers down the western slope and reached the Pacific Ocean in early November 1805.

On the return trip, near Lolo Pass, Lewis and Clark split the party into two groups. Lewis went northeast, and Clark traveled southeast to explore the Yellowstone River. Six weeks later, they reunited near the mouth of the Yellowstone. They returned to St. Louis on September 23, 1806, having traveled 8,000 miles (12,800 kilometers) and having spent only $38,000, not including their fee.

Trading Posts

The stories told by expedition members about the vast numbers of fur-bearing animals that they had seen brought a wave of trappers

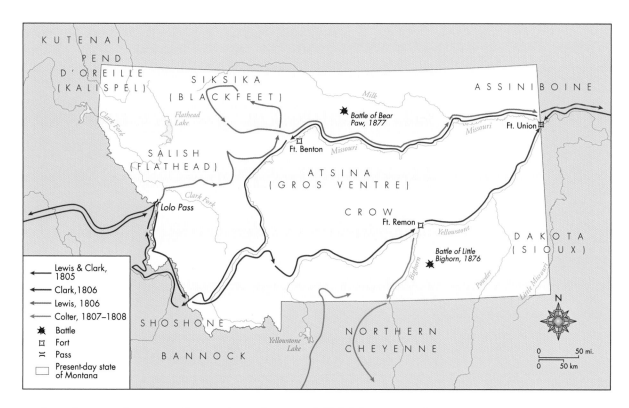

Map legend:
- Lewis & Clark, 1805
- Clark, 1806
- Lewis, 1806
- Colter, 1807–1808
- ✳ Battle
- ⌂ Fort
- ≍ Pass
- ☐ Present-day state of Montana

Map labels: KUTENAI, PEND D'OREILLE (KALISPEL), SIKSIKA (BLACKFEET), ASSINIBOINE, Milk, Battle of Bear Paw, 1877, Missouri, Ft. Union, Flathead Lake, Clark Fork, SALISH (FLATHEAD), Ft. Benton, Missouri, ATSINA (GROS VENTRE), CROW, Clark Fork, Lolo Pass, Ft. Remon, Yellowstone, DAKOTA (SIOUX), Battle of Little Bighorn, 1876, Bighorn, Powder, Little Missouri, SHOSHONE, Yellowstone Lake, NORTHERN CHEYENNE, BANNOCK, N, 0 50 mi., 0 50 km

and traders to the area. Soon, American and British companies began to settle east of the Continental Divide.

The first fur-trading post was Fort Remon, better known as Fort Manuel Lisa. In 1807, trader Manuel Lisa established the fort at the mouth of the Bighorn River near present-day Billings as part of his Missouri Fur Company. Traders from Fort Remon, including Jim Bridger, Jedediah Smith, and others mapped trails and stabilized the fur trade with most of the Native American tribes.

John Jacob Astor's American Fur Company established Fort Union along the Missouri River in 1829. After Fort Union was established, the American Fur Company dominated Montana's fur trade.

Fort Union

In 1828, John Jacob Astor sent Kenneth McKenzie to build Fort Union. It became the center of the fur trade for all of eastern Montana.

The Crow, the Blackfeet, and the Assiniboine were among the Plains tribes drawn to the fort. They traded beaver pelts, buffalo hides, and elk skins.

The fort prospered under McKenzie. It became the most elegant place to stay west of St. Louis, Missouri. Crystal goblets, French wines, and servants dressed in fine uniforms lured many famous visitors, including explorer Jim Bridger, Prince Maximilian of Germany, and artist John James Audubon. ■

John Colter of the Missouri Fur Company and Canadian David Thompson of the North West Company did most of the exploration and mapping of Montana. In 1807–1808, Colter, who had been a member of the Lewis and Clark Expedition, discovered the land that is now Yellowstone National Park.

Up the Missouri River from Fort Union, Fort Benton, established in 1846 as Fort Lewis, came to be known as the "birthplace of Montana." More than 600 steamboats arrived at the fort between 1859 and the 1870s, making it the world's most remote inland port. Built by Astor's American Fur Company, Fort Benton also served as trailhead for the Mullan Road, which linked Montana with Fort Walla Walla in Washington. Of all the trading posts built during the beaver-pelt trading era, only Fort Benton still exists.

Fort Benton in the 1860s

In the mid-1800s, the pelt trade diminished as a result of a change in European fashions and the devastation of the area's beaver population. Interest in tanned buffalo hides for clothing and saddles kept some forts open. Hunters and skinners flooded the Plains and slaughtered millions of buffalo. They took only the hides, leaving the carcasses to rot.

Missionaries

Some Iroquois who accompanied French traders to western Montana in the early 1800s stayed and married Kutenai and Flathead women. Because most of the traders were Catholic, they taught local tribes about Christianity.

As a result of this initial contact, Father Pierre Jean de Smet came to Montana in 1841 and established St. Mary's Mission in Bitterroot Valley near present-day Montana. He taught the

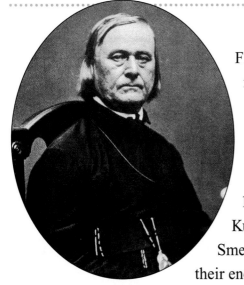

Flathead Indians there about Christianity, farming, and irrigation. Father Anthony Ravalli later started a sawmill, as well as a gristmill for grinding grains into flour. St. Mary's became a trading post in 1850.

In 1844, Father de Smet helped establish St. Ignatius's mission. It was built near Flathead Lake in 1854 to serve the Pend d'Oreille, the Flathead, and the Kutenai. The Flathead became disillusioned with Father de Smet, however, when he began his missionary work with their enemies, the Blackfeet.

Father Pierre Jean de Smet was one of the missionaries who came to Montana in the 1800s.

Gold Fever and Lawlessness

In 1849, the California gold rush brought prospectors to Montana's Rocky Mountains. In 1858, James and Granville Stuart found gold on Gold Creek, between Drummond and Deer Lodge. In 1862, bigger strikes on Grasshopper Creek, Alder Gulch, and Last Chance Gulch, in southwestern Montana, attracted many adventurers.

The mining towns of Bannack, Virginia City, and Helena thrived. Bozeman and Missoula also prospered as supply centers for mining communities.

With the increased population and rampant "gold fever" came lawlessness. People of all types came to make their fortunes. Some worked hard and earned it, but others came to steal it. Incidents ranged from minor thefts to brutal murders.

Citizens of Virginia City, trying to bring law and order to their town, hired Henry Plummer as their sheriff. Plummer had different plans, however. He secretly led a gang of thieves, who were known as the Innocents and had killed more than 100 people.

Calamity Jane (ca. 1852–1903)

"Calamity Jane" was born Martha Jane Canary in 1852 in Princeton, Missouri. She arrived in Virginia City, Montana, with her parents, sometime during the 1865 gold rush. During her life, she was a prostitute, an army scout, and a prospector. She claimed to have been a scout for Lieutenant Colonel George Armstrong Custer, the wife of Wild Bill Hickok, and the mother of Hickok's daughter. Because she was such a notorious liar, it is difficult to verify many of her claims. Her life ended in poverty in 1903. According to her wishes, friends laid her to rest next to Wild Bill in Deadwood, South Dakota. ■

When the truth came out about the Plummer gang in December 1863, men from Bannack and Virginia City formed their own group to solve the problem. Operating outside the law, they hunted down, tried, and hanged twenty-one men, including Plummer.

Trails to Fertile Land

Gold wasn't the only thing that brought people to Montana in the 1860s. Many came because of the fertile land.

Settlers traveled along four main routes. The Fisk Wagon Trail across northern Montana connected St. Paul, Minnesota, with Fort Benton. This 624-mile (1,004-km) trail joined Mullan Road, which crossed the Continental Divide and traveled west to Fort Walla Walla in Washington. In southern Montana, the Bozeman Trail veered off the famous Oregon Trail and brought settlers to Virginia City. The Corinne Road ran from Helena South to Corinne, Utah. Many of these trails crossed Indian lands guaranteed by treaty, and local tribes became hostile toward white settlers. Military forts and outposts were built to restore order and ensure the settlers' safe passage.

Settlers arriving in Helena

Territorial Days

Before 1863, various U.S. territories governed the area now called Montana. The land east of the Continental Divide was part of the Louisiana Purchase from 1803 to 1812, Missouri Territory from 1812 to 1821, an unorganized territory called Indian Country from 1821 to 1854, Nebraska Territory from 1854 to 1861, and Dakota Territory from 1861 to 1863. The land west of the Continental Divide belonged to Great Britain until 1846 (but was also claimed by the United States as part of Oregon Country), Oregon Territory from 1848 to 1853, and Washington Territory from 1853 to 1863.

Idaho Territory was established in 1863. This vast territory included nearly all of present-day Montana. In 1864, Sydney Edgerton, chief justice of Idaho Territory, lobbied in Washington, D.C., for a separate Montana Territory. On May 26, 1864, Congress passed the Organic Act, which separated Montana from Idaho, and President Abraham Lincoln approved it.

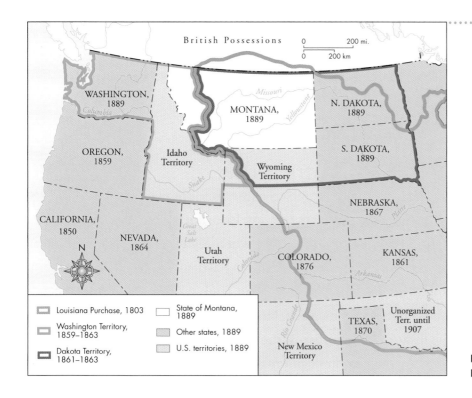

Historical map of
Montana

Sydney Edgerton was
the first governor of
Montana Territory.

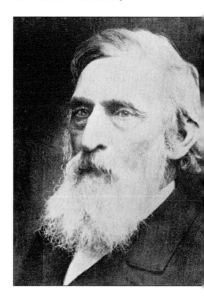

In December 1864, the newly formed Montana Territory held its first territorial assembly in Bannack, the territorial capital. Delegates met for sixty days, passed 700 pages of laws, and voted to move the capital to Virginia City.

Anger and confusion characterized early politics in Montana Territory. As in other states during the Civil War (1861–1865), pro-Union and pro-Confederate groups argued about almost every issue. Territorial power rested in the hands of appointed Union Republicans such as the first governor, Sydney Edgerton.

Interest in statehood began with supporters of Thomas Meagher, the Democratic territorial secretary. In April 1866, while Governor Edgerton was away, acting governor Meagher called a constitutional convention and produced a written constitution. This first Montana constitution was lost, apparently on the way to the printer in St. Louis. Meagher died mysteriously later that year. Support for statehood waned until the 1870s, when political calm returned.

The Great Cattle Drive

Stockmen originally raised cattle in Montana to feed the hungry miners who came to the region to strike it rich. The first big cattle operation began in 1850, when Richard Grant and his sons James and Johnny began buying worn-out cattle from wagon trains traveling along the Oregon Trail. After they fattened the cattle on rich Montana grass, the Grants traded with the settlers—one healthy animal for two skinny ones.

In 1866, another cattleman, Nelson Story, brought 1,000 longhorn cattle from Texas and settled in Paradise and Gallatin Valleys.

Granville Stuart (1834–1918)

Granville Stuart, born into a Scottish family in West Virginia, first set foot in Montana on his way home from the California gold rush. He and his brother discovered gold on Gold Creek and began Montana's own gold rush in 1857. In 1862, Stuart set up a store in Bannack, supplying goods to hundreds of desperate miners. He established a ranch in Deer Lodge Valley and later the DHS Ranch east of Lewistown.

Granville Stuart served on Montana's territorial council. Elected president of the Montana Stockgrowers Association in 1884, he represented ranchers who were angry with cattle rustlers, people who steal cattle. Hundreds of cattle rustlers were roaming the eastern Montana area. When the government and the U.S. Army failed to solve the problem, Stuart and other ranchers formed Stuart's Stranglers. Acting on its own, the group hunted down and hanged 25 to 100 suspected cattle rustlers in 1884. ■

He bought cheap cattle from Texas, drove them north for the summer, grazed them on Montana's abundant grasslands, and then shipped them to market in the East.

Driving cattle from Texas to the Montana plains

Fattened steers were sometimes driven south into Wyoming to Union Pacific railheads. When the Northern Pacific line was built in Montana along the Yellowstone River in 1881–1882, Miles City, Billings, and Wibaux became centers for the livestock trade.

Montana's open range was short-lived, however. The summer of 1886 was one of the driest on record. With little to eat and diminishing water supplies, the cattle weakened. The winter of 1886–1887 was extremely cold, and most of Montana's cattle perished. The great cattle-drive era was over.

Indian Trouble

White settlers in wagon trains destroyed much of the area's game animals and angered Native Americans by repeatedly breaking treaties. Most tribes, including the Flathead, the Blackfeet, and the Crow, resigned themselves to the superior military power of the settlers and soldiers and settled peacefully on reservations—but several Plains tribes resisted. Dakota and Cheyenne warriors attacked wagon trains, raided settlements, and stole cattle and horses.

A series of battles followed in the 1870s between Plains Indian war parties and U.S. Army posts established throughout the territory. This ongoing struggle culminated in some of the most famous Indian battles in American history—the Battle of Little Bighorn and the pursuit and capture of Chief Joseph and the Nez Perce.

The Battle of Little Bighorn

On the morning of June 25, 1876, Lieutenant Colonel George Armstrong Custer led a force of 600 men into the Valley of the Little Bighorn in southeastern Montana. Custer's troops, part of a larger force under the command of General Alfred H. Terry, had been sent to battle the Dakota and Cheyenne. Meanwhile, the Dakota had left their reservation in Dakota Territory in search of food and moved west to join the Cheyenne in Montana.

Custer's scouts located Dakota and Cheyenne camps along the Little Bighorn River, but Custer was unaware that several thousand warriors awaited him. He separated his troops into three groups and remained with one of them. The two other groups went into action but were quickly pinned down.

General Custer at the
Battle of Little Bighorn

Meanwhile, Custer's force of about 200 men met the full strength of the experienced Dakota and Cheyenne warriors. Outnumbered, Custer and every one of his men were killed. Indian reports of the battle revealed that many of Custer's men committed suicide rather than be taken hostage by Dakota chief Sitting Bull.

Sitting Bull was a
leader of the Dakota
Indians.

Although Sitting Bull, Crazy Horse, and other Indian leaders won a strategic victory at Little Bighorn, their glory was short-lived. News of the massacre brought a national call for revenge. The U.S. War Department dispatched one-third of the U.S. Army to Montana. Custer's so-called Last Stand was also a last stand for the Plains Indians. In only a few years, starvation and military force moved the remaining members of the once-proud Plains tribes onto reservations.

Little Bighorn Battlefield National Monument

The site of one of the most famous battles in the history of the West— the Battle of Little Bighorn—is located 15 miles (24 km) southeast of Hardin. Visiting the stark, silent landscape of the Valley of the Little Bighorn today is a moving experience. Simple stone markers on the vast open prairie show where Custer's men fell. The battlefield's name was changed from Custer Battlefield to the Little Bighorn Battlefield National Monument to recognize both sides in the conflict. ■

Chief Joseph and the Nez Perce

Two of the most famous Indian battles in Montana history involved a tribe that was not native to the state. In the 1860s and 1870s, white ranchers planned to settle the Nez Perce homeland, centered in Wallowa Valley in southeastern Oregon. The federal government tried to force the Nez Perce to settle on an Idaho reservation, but they refused. After skirmishes in 1877, five bands of Nez Perce— some 800 people—fled eastward, hoping for help from the Crow as they made their way to Canada.

Once in Montana, the Nez Perce camped on the western side of Big Hole Valley, west of Wisdom. Early on the morning of August 9, 1877, cavalry forces surprised the Nez Perce. After driving the soldiers into a wooded knoll across the river, a group of Nez Perce pinned them down for twenty-four hours, allowing the rest of their tribe to escape.

After fleeing through what is now Yellowstone National Park, the Nez Perce turned north toward Canada. U.S. troops caught up with them 16 miles (26 km) north of present-day Chinook. Several days of fierce fighting followed in the Battle of

Chief Joseph

Bears Paw. Outnumbered and outgunned, the Nez Perce finally agreed to lay down their arms.

At his surrender following the Battle of Bears Paw, Chief Joseph delivered one of the most famous and stirring speeches in American history. He said, "It is cold and we have no blankets. The little children are freezing to death. . . . I want to have time to look for my children and see how many of them I can find. Maybe I shall find them among the dead. Hear me, my chiefs. I am tired; my heart is sick and sad. From where the sun now stands, I will fight no more forever."

According to the terms of their surrender, Chief Joseph and the Nez Perce believed they could return to their homeland in Oregon. Instead, the tribe was sent to Oklahoma. They were not allowed to return to the Northwest until 1885.

The Move to Statehood

After the chaos and bloodshed of the 1860s and 1870s, Montana Territory petitioned the federal government for statehood. In 1884, a second constitutional convention took place in Helena, the territorial capital since 1875. The resulting document failed to win Congress's approval, however. In 1889, Congress finally passed an act permitting the territory to write another constitution and apply again for statehood.

A third constitutional convention was convened in Helena in July 1889. After six weeks of debate, a constitution was written, patterned after constitutions of other western states. It was approved on October 1, 1889. President Benjamin Harrison proclaimed Montana the forty-first state on November 8, 1889. Joseph K. Toole of Helena became the first governor of the new state.

Joseph K. Toole, first governor of the state of Montana

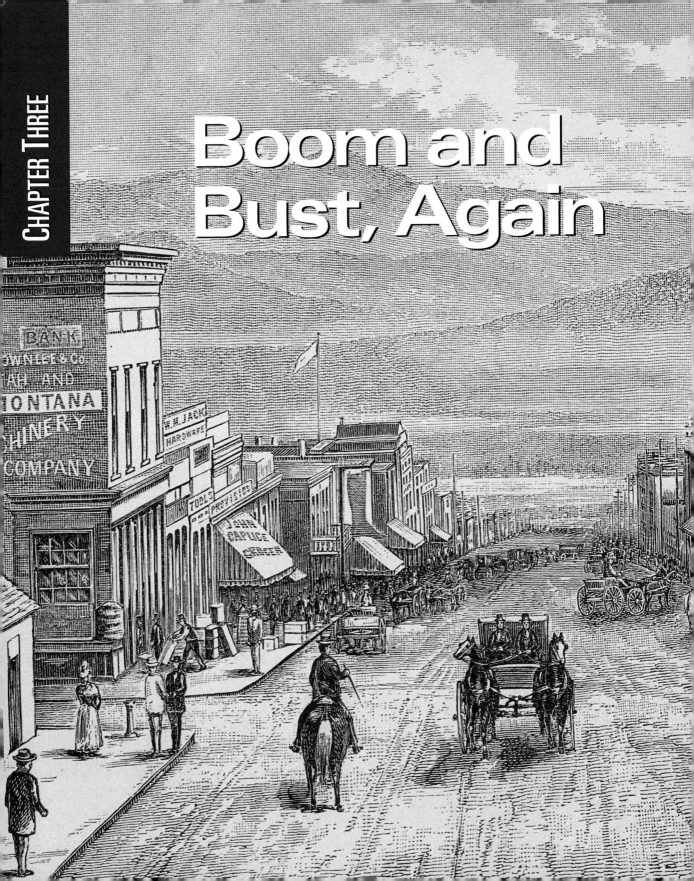

CHAPTER THREE

Boom and Bust, Again

The Chicago, Milwaukee, and St. Paul Railway Company expanded into Montana in 1909.

By the time Montana entered the Union, its population had grown to 142,924. Corporate mining, a homestead boom, and turbulent politics dominated the state's first forty years. Communities grew along three major rail lines in Montana.

The Northern Pacific was the first rail line to cross the state. In 1883, it celebrated its transcontinental connection with a ceremony near Gold Creek, just west of Helena. The government gave Northern Pacific land for every mile of track it laid—a total of about 17 million acres (6.9 million hectares).

In 1887, the Great Northern Railroad stretched from Minot, North Dakota, to Great Falls. James J. Hill's crew of 9,000 finished a 550-mile (885-km) line. Later construction and acquisitions gave Hill almost complete control of rail shipping from Seattle, Washington, to the Great Lakes.

In 1909, the Chicago, Milwaukee, and St. Paul Railway Company completed tracks through central Montana. It was the first long-distance electrified rail span in America.

Each of these rail lines spawned farming and mining communities and created a demand for coal. Their main function was transporting minerals to markets in the East. Much of the state's mineral wealth in the 1880s and 1890s came from the area around Butte. Gold and then silver came from the rocky ledges of Butte Hill,

Opposite: Butte in the 1890s

Butte Hill was once called the "richest hill on earth."

James J. Hill (1838–1916)

Born near Rockwood, Ontario, in Canada, James J. Hill founded the Great Northern Railway in 1890. By 1893, the railway extended from Lake Superior across the northern states to Puget Sound, Washington. It was the first transcontinental railroad built without government money. Hill was an outstanding financier, philanthropist, orator, and writer. ▪

which was called the "richest hill on earth." Huge deposits of copper—used by the electrical industry—added to the region's prosperity. This began the era known as the War of the Copper Kings.

The Copper Kings

In the final decades of the nineteenth century, three men dominated the state of Montana—William A. Clark, Marcus Daly, and F. Augustus Heinze. The so-called Copper Kings came to Montana with remarkable business sense, financial backing, and enormous ambition.

Born in Pennsylvania in 1839, William A. Clark came to Bannack seeking gold in 1863. He moved to Deer Lodge, became a banker, and invested in several local mines. Clark made his fortune buying old silver mines and mining copper. His financial empire eventually included forty-six mines, supply stores, transportation companies, banks, ore-processing plants, and real estate. By 1890, his influence was so extensive that he was cited as one of the 100 men who "owned America."

Clark was also interested in politics. After several unsuccessful tries, Clark finally won a seat in the U.S. Senate in 1899. He later resigned, but was reelected in 1901.

Marcus Daly came from Ireland in 1856. A mining company in Utah sent him to investigate a silver mine near Butte. He invested his own money in the venture and eventually bought the Anaconda Mine, which produced millions of pounds of nearly pure copper. Daly established the town of Anaconda near his mines and lobbied to have Anaconda named the state capital. After a hard-fought, corrupt political campaign between Daly and his rival Clark, Helena was given the honor of being named state capitol.

The feud between Daly and Clark, called the War of the Copper Kings, reached legendary extremes. The dispute was thought to have begun over a remark Clark had made slighting Daly. The dispute continued until Daly's death in 1900.

The third Copper King, F. Augustus Heinze, was the son of wealthy German immigrants. He came to Butte as a mining engineer around 1890, and he soon owned several mines and an ore-smelting plant.

Heinze joined forces with William Clark to head off the efforts of Standard Oil Company's Amalgamated Copper Company to control the copper-mining industry. By the 1890s, Standard Oil, established in 1870 by John D. Rockefeller, had become one of the largest and most powerful companies in the United States.

Heinze amassed a sizable fortune by manipulating state mining laws and influencing local courts, but he was unable to fight off the

William Andrews Clark became a wealthy man in Montana.

Marcus Daly owned the Anaconda Mine.

vast Standard Oil empire. After buying Daly's holdings, Standard purchased Clark's and Heinze's mining interests.

As each of the Copper Kings sold out to Standard Oil, the company's power grew. Standard Oil, known as the Anaconda Company in Montana, and the Montana Power Company controlled almost the entire state. This corporate control led to labor disputes over poor working conditions for miners. Labor unions, such as the Western Federation of Miners, established in 1893, moved in. Soon Butte became the most unionized city in the United States. Attempts to control the excesses of the powerful corporations met with limited success, however.

An advertisement for the Northern Pacific Railway

Attracting Homesteaders

The remoteness of the plains prevented settlement until the early 1900s. Railroad entrepreneurs such as James J. Hill recognized the benefits of establishing communities along railroads. Towns meant passengers, freight, and a steady supply of employees.

Hill and others launched advertising campaigns along the eastern seaboard, hoping to attract immigrants with the promise of free land. They sent brochures to Europe, extolling the virtues of Montana's plains. Many of their claims, such as fertile soil, abundant rainfall, and mild winters, were exaggerated. Some were outright lies.

These fanciful promises and the Enlarged Homestead Act of 1909 brought a boom in the state's population. Thousands flocked to Montana to claim the 320 acres (130 ha) per adult that the act promised. By 1910, the number of farms in the state had doubled, and the state's population had increased 60 percent.

As good as it sounded, 320 acres of Great Plains land was not enough to support an average family unless weather conditions were perfect—and they seldom were. In 1918, disaster struck. Overcultivation, from supplying wheat for the troops during World War I (1914–1918), and an extreme drought, ruined most farms. Farmers could not repay their debts. More than half had to give up their land. Montana and North Dakota were the only two states to reduce their populations during the 1920s. Even now, the eastern plains are not as heavily populated as they were in 1918.

Drought conditions, falling crop prices, and bank failures turned Montana's agricultural boom into a bust. Although new railroads and dams for irrigation and electric power in central Montana were being built, little could help the struggling farmers of the eastern plains.

The Great Depression

The state's economic conditions worsened during the Great Depression (1929–1939). The depression years were a period of extreme financial hardship for the people of the United States. Businesses closed, and people lost their jobs. Fewer factories produced fewer goods, and demand for Montana's raw materials—lumber and minerals—dropped dramatically. Cattle and wheat prices fell. Farmers could not even pay the freight to get their produce to

Fort Peck Dam

Fort Peck Dam is one of the world's largest earth-fill dams. It interrupts the flow of the Missouri River in northeastern Montana, creating Fort Peck Lake.

Named for a Native American trading post built in 1867, Fort Peck Dam was built during the Great Depression as part of President Franklin D. Roosevelt's New Deal program. The dam cost more than $150 million to build and employed 50,000 workers.

When it was completed in 1940, it spanned more than 3 miles (5 km) and created the world's largest reservoir. Fort Peck Lake is still the third-largest man-made reservoir in the world. ■

market. Widespread unemployment swept the lumber, mining, and agricultural industries.

In the early 1930s, President Franklin Roosevelt responded with a program of economic recovery that included huge public-works projects. New Deal projects put people back to work and improved public services. The largest tax-funded project in the state was the Fort Peck Dam on the Missouri River.

The New Deal funded hundreds of other public-works projects in Montana. Rural electrification brought power to remote farms.

Forty Civilian Conservation Corps (CCC) camps put 25,600 people to work planting evergreen trees in reforestation projects. CCC laborers also worked on Going-to-the-Sun Highway in Glacier National Park, soil-conservation projects, insect control, and the construction of parks and recreation areas.

War Efforts

In 1941, the United States entered World War II (1939–1945). A dramatic increase in the demand for Montana's natural resources put Montana to work. Metals, lumber, and food crops were needed in the war effort. Coal, petroleum, and copper were especially in demand. Weather conditions cooperated during the 1940s, allowing Montana's farmers and ranchers to recover from decades of hardship.

World War II also brought Montana's only military installations. Malmstrom Air Force Base, near Great Falls, was built as a transit base for war materials being shipped to the former Soviet Union. Glasgow Air Force Base also boosted local population and stimulated business in eastern Montana until it closed in 1969.

Loading coal in Colstrip

Mike Mansfield (1903–)

Raised in Great Falls, Mike Mansfield worked as a miner in Butte and as a college history professor. In 1942, he was elected to the U.S. House of Representatives. He also served as Democratic Majority Leader in the Senate from 1961 to 1977. A powerful member of the Senate Foreign Relations Committee, his voice greatly influenced national policy.

At seventy-three, Mansfield retired and was appointed ambassador to Japan, a post he held until 1988. Mansfield coauthored the Twenty-Sixth Amendment to the U.S. Constitution, which made eighteen the legal age to vote. ■

CHAPTER FOUR

A Time of Change

Montana's north-central plains

The last half of the twentieth century brought more ups and downs to Montana. During this period, there was a shift in importance from western Montana and its logging and mining industries to the eastern plains. Coal, oil, and gas resources replaced gold, silver, copper, and timber as the state's main industries, and concern for the state's environment increased.

In the 1950s, Montana's largest corporation, the Anaconda Company, struggled with a postwar drop in demand for copper. In 1955, near Butte, the company began open-pit mining—excavating huge pits to extract valuable minerals below the surface. Cheaper and faster than traditional underground mining, open-pit mining requires a smaller workforce. Many Montanans opposed the technique for environmental reasons. For example, the Anaconda Company's Berkeley Pit, which opened new reserves of

Opposite: The Bridger Mountains near Bozeman

low-grade copper ore, grew so large that the entire neighborhood of Meaderville demolished.

Open-pit mining revived Anaconda's copper mining until the 1970s. By then, fiber-optic cable began replacing copper wire in phone lines, and world competition lessened Anaconda's power in the industry. Environmental laws also became stricter.

By 1977, the Anaconda Company had sold all its mining and smelting interests around Butte to oil giant Atlantic Richfield Company (ARCO). ARCO closed most of its smelter and refinery operations in 1980 and its mining operations soon after. Having dominated Montana's politics and media for a century, the Anaconda Company had finally shut down.

Strip Mining and Oil Drilling

Almost since the arrival of the state's first settlers, coal has been mined in Montana. The large-scale operations had to wait for the arrival of railroads, however. For years, the areas around Red Lodge, Great Falls, Colstrip, and Roundup were quite active.

When trains converted to electricity, coal production declined. Then, improvements were made in coal-mining machinery, and interest in coal-powered electrical generating plants increased. Vast coal fields in southeastern Montana became more accessible.

By the 1970s, strip-mining—the process of scooping up tons of earth to expose layers of coal, harvesting the coal, and returning the rock and soil—became the accepted method of coal mining. Complaints of environmental destruction forced mining companies to replant the ground where coal had been mined.

The 1970s saw the construction of four electric generators near Colstrip, even though local citizens, environmental groups, and Native Americans opposed the project. Power from these coal-burning generators was marketed on the West Coast. The energy crisis of the 1970s spurred a dramatic increase in coal production—nearly 40 million tons of coal were mined a year, up from 3 million tons a year in the 1960s.

Oil and gas production increased dramatically in the 1950s after new reserves, such as those at Williston Basin, were discovered in eastern Montana. Oil drilling began as early as 1915, but it took new fields and increased demand to make petroleum the state's leading mineral. The worldwide energy crunch of the 1970s benefited refineries in Billings, Baker, Broadus, and Sidney.

The Bridger Canyon Stallion Ranch

Changes on the Farm

Farming and ranching operations in Montana, mostly family-owned, have always had roller-coaster profitability. Machines, fewer farmworkers, and larger farms have changed the way Montana farmers work. Only hardworking, diversified operations have survived. Although the national trend has been toward specialization, or one-crop farms, many Montana

Yellowstone Fires

During the summer of 1988, park officials, environmentalists, and tourists were concerned by the extreme drought in Yellowstone National Park. In July, lightning sparked extensive forest fires throughout the park, destroying hundreds of thousands of acres. Although wildflowers blanket the hillsides and wildlife thrives in the park, many who have seen the area before the fires are disheartened at the scope of the destruction that claimed so many thousands of acres of majestic trees. Fire is part of the natural cycle of the forest, but many generations will pass before nature replaces everything that was lost. ■

farmers and ranchers have had to diversify and raise a variety of crops and livestock.

Productive years between 1960 and the early 1970s led to an increase in land values and record rates of production. Encouraged by these trends, farmers and ranchers borrowed heavily to upgrade equipment and expand operations. Unfortunately, another drought hit in the late 1970s and early 1980s.

Irrigation projects and water-conservation programs have played a role in Montana's agricultural survival. Projects on the Milk, Missouri, and Lower Yellowstone Rivers, including four dams at Great Falls and Hungry Horse Dam northeast of Kalispell, provide needed water for crops and hydroelectric power.

Appreciating Montana's Nature

The decades of unrestricted mining and logging operations have damaged Montana's environment. Beginning in the 1970s, the state set environmental policies, such as the Montana Environmental Policy Act. The 1970s and 1980s saw some improvement in air and water quality. In the 1990s, however, some deterioration took place, even with the support of many of the state's citizens.

Life in the urbanized areas of the United States has become more hectic, and social issues continue to smolder. For those reasons, the open spaces, sparse population, and relative isolation of Montana attract a variety of people, from tourists to celebrities. Actors who find peace along the streams of Montana, away from the public and the press, include Michael Keaton, Brooke Shields, Tom Cruise, and Nicole Kidman, to name just a few.

The Rise of Radical Groups

In some cases, people come to the western states because they hold antigovernment and other extreme, antisocial beliefs. They want to live as far from government authority as possible. A few of these groups have settled in Montana, mostly near the Idaho border. Though small in number, their influence—through Internet sites and publications—is cause for concern. Two such groups are the Freemen Movement and the Militia of Montana.

In 1994, John Trochmann, with his brother David and his nephew Randy, founded the Militia of Montana in Noxon. In its publication *Taking Aim,* the group urges its readers to arm themselves with assault rifles, train in guerrilla-warfare tactics, and form secret "cells" of antigovernment activists.

In 1996, the Freemen Movement brought notoriety to the town of Jordan in eastern Montana during a siege by agents of the Federal Bureau of Investigation (FBI). The group maintained a large arsenal of weapons on the ranch of a local sympathizer. Defying federal authority, it established its own government and currency. Members refused to pay taxes, issued millions of dollars in money orders, and threatened the lives of local officials.

The FBI intervened in the summer of 1996. It arrested the group's leaders and surrounded the ranch. Agents turned off elec-

The Unabomber

Disturbed individuals sometimes seek refuge in wilderness areas. One such man was Theodore Kaczynski, who was trying to escape a world he believed was evil and controlled by technology. He moved to a small cabin near Lincoln, Montana, where he constructed letter bombs and mailed them to individuals throughout America. His bombs killed three people and injured about two dozen. In 1996, the so-called Unabomber was captured after his brother recognized Kaczynski's writing style and extreme ideas in a multipage manifesto published in national newspapers. In 1998, Kaczynski pled guilty to some of the bombings and was sentenced to life imprisonment without possibility of parole. ■

tricity and telephone service. After eighty-one days, the group surrendered, and sixteen men, women, and children were arrested.

Looking to the Future

In 1998, Montana governor Marc Racicot addressed the press about the rise of radical groups in the state. He emphasized that the vast majority of Montana's citizens are law-abiding, friendly, and eager to welcome people to the state.

Montanans are proud of their state's past and natural beauty. They expect great advances in the quality of life for its citizens and visitors.

CHAPTER FIVE

Big Sky Country

The Absaroka
Mountain Range

Montana, the fourth-largest state, is located in the north-western United States. It is bordered on the north by the Canadian provinces of British Columbia, Alberta, and Saskatchewan, on the east by North Dakota and South Dakota, on the south by Wyoming, and on the south and west by Idaho.

The vast Big Sky Country covers 147,046 square miles (380,849 sq km), including 1,490 square miles (3,859 sq km) of inland water. The state's highest point is Granite Peak, west of Red Lodge at 12,799 feet (3,904 meters) above sea level. Montana's lowest point is 1,800 feet (549 m) above sea level along the Kootenai River in Lincoln County.

Eastern Montana is made up of vast prairies and small mountain ranges. Seas of waving prairie grass and a virtually unobstructed view of the crystal blue sky gives the state its most popular nickname—Big Sky Country.

Opposite: A rainbow
over a farm near
Billings

To the west, gently rolling high plains give way to the Rocky Mountains. The western part of the state is spectacular, with rocky peaks, grassy meadows, and thick pine and fir forests.

Geologic History

During the Paleozoic Era (240 to 570 million years ago), Montana was a flat plain, sometimes flooded by shallow seas. The Rocky Mountains began forming about 70 million to 90 million years ago.

Seas again covered parts of the region during the Mesozoic Era, which ended 65 million years ago. Thick layers of sediment eventually hardened to rock. Many species of dinosaurs roamed the area during the Paleozoic and Mesozoic Eras, leaving behind fossilized bones and nests of fossilized eggs.

In eastern Montana, isolated mountain ranges dot the landscape. About 50 million years ago, volcanoes erupted and lava rose to the surface. Great swamps filled, then dried up, compacting layers of vegetation into huge deposits of coal.

The great Pleistocene ice ages, about 2 million years ago, blanketed much of Montana in ice and snow. This was a period of bit-

Glacier National Park

Glacier National Park opened in 1910. In 1932, it combined with Canada's Waterton Lakes National Park to form the world's first international park, Waterton–Glacier International Peace Park, to honor the friendship shared by the United States and Canada.

The largest glacier in the park is Grinnell Glacier. Other glaciers include Gem, Salamander, and Sperry. The most unusual glacier in the park is Grasshopper Glacier, so named because it contains the frozen remains of millions of a now-extinct grasshopper species. ▨

ter cold and winter snowfalls so great that the snow did not melt during summer. Huge glaciers formed in the Rocky Mountains and along the northern plains. Their movement formed lakes, carved valleys, and shaped mountains. Smaller glaciers can still be seen in Glacier National Park.

The Rocky Mountains

Montana has two major regions—the Rocky Mountains in the west and southwest and the Great Plains in the center and east. The Rocky Mountain region is sometimes divided into the northern Rocky Mountains and the middle Rocky Mountains.

A northwest-southeast line divides Montana's western Rocky Mountains from the rest of the state. More than fifty mountain ranges rise within this region. The most important ranges include the Absaroka, Beartooth, Big Belt, Bitterroot, Bridger, Cabinet,

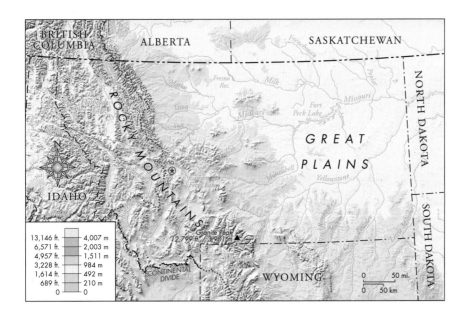

Montana's topography

The Beartooth Mountains are part of Montana's Rocky Mountain region.

Flathead, Gallatin, Madison, Mission, Ruby, Swan, and Tobacco Root. A few peaks exceed 12,000 feet (3,660 m) but most range from 6,000 to 10,000 feet (1,830 to 3,050 m). The state's highest point, Granite Peak, is in the Beartooth Range in south-central Montana.

The long, roughly parallel mountain chains of western Montana are covered with forests, lakes, river basins, and valleys. In the northwestern part of the state, valleys are narrow and rugged, but the southwest has broad, grassy valleys up to 40 miles (64 km) wide.

The Continental Divide, the dividing line between the Pacific and Atlantic watersheds, enters Montana from the north in Glacier

National Park. It follows the crests of various mountain ranges to the south, then turns west near Butte. At Lost Trail Pass, west of Wisdom, it turns south again and follows the Bitterroot and Beaverhead Ranges, forming part of Montana's border with Idaho.

The Great Plains

The topography of the eastern part of Montana is more consistent than the Rocky Mountain region. Elevations range from 2,000 to 3,300 feet (610 to 1,007 m). It features semiarid, or dry, landforms, including mesas, buttes, gullies, canyons, and badlands.

Red cliffs of the Terry Badlands

Montana's Geographical Features

Total area; rank	147,046 sq. mi. (380,849 sq km); 4th
Land; rank	145,556 sq. mi. (376,990 sq km); 4th
Water; rank	1,490 sq. mi. (3,859 sq km); 19th
Inland water; rank	1,490 sq. mi. (3,859 sq km); 15th
Geographic center	8 miles (13 km) west of Lewistown
Highest point	Granite Peak, 12,799 feet (3,904 m)
Lowest point	1,800 feet (549 m) above sea level along the Kootenai River in Lincoln County
Largest city	Billings
Population; rank	803,655 (1990 census); 44th
Record high temperature	117°F (47°C) at Glendive on July 20, 1893, and at Medicine Lake on July 5, 1937
Record low temperature	–70°F (–57°C) at Rogers Pass on January 20, 1954
Average July temperature	68°F (20°C)
Average January temperature	18°F (–8°C)
Average annual precipitation	15 inches (38 cm)

The plains section, sometimes called the Missouri Plateau, divides into two distinct areas. The northern plains, once covered with glaciers, have more scattered lakes and rougher terrain. Southern sections are drier and smoother. Although scattered mountain ranges dot the region, it is mostly open grassland. Sweetgrass, Big Snowy, Bears Paw, Little Rocky, and Crazy Mountains rise in the Missouri Plateau.

Rivers and Lakes

Montana is the only state from which water drains through river systems to three oceans: the Atlantic Ocean (by way of the Gulf of Mexico), the Pacific Ocean, and the Arctic Ocean (by way of Hudson Bay) in northern Canada. A small area in the north-central part of the state drains north by way of the Belly, Saint Mary, and Waterton Rivers. West of the Continental Divide, the Kootenai, Clark Fork, and Flathead Rivers join the Columbia River system, flowing westward.

Montana's most important river is the Missouri, which flows eastward across the state. Its source at Three Forks merges the Jefferson, Gallatin, and Madison Rivers. The Milk, Musselshell, Sun, Poplar, and Judith Rivers join the Missouri. Just east of the Montana–North Dakota border, the Missouri meets its largest tributary,

The Upper Missouri River near Fort Benton

the Yellowstone, which enters Montana from Wyoming and flows northeast across the Great Plains.

Montana has hundreds of natural and man-made lakes. The largest natural lake, Flathead Lake, covers 189 square miles (490 sq km) in a mountain valley south of Glacier National Park. The largest man-made lake in Montana is Fort Peck Lake, 383 square miles (992 sq km). It formed when the Missouri River was dammed in the 1930s. Fort Peck Dam and facilities on the Yellowstone River provide hydroelectric power and irrigation for dry regions of eastern Montana.

Aspen trees in the fall

Plant Life

Most of Montana's plains are treeless, covered with natural grasses such as buffalo and blue grama. Drier areas are covered with cacti, bunchgrass, and low-growing shrubs such as sagebrush. Along river valleys and in upland areas, willow, poplar, and cottonwood trees grow. At higher altitudes in the west, forests of ponderosa pine, lodgepole pine, Douglas fir, juniper, larch, spruce, and red cedar thrive. About one-fourth of the state is forested.

Throughout Montana, wildflowers grow in profusion. From the prairies and grass-lands of the east to the forests and alpine meadows of the west, springtime brings colorful displays of brown-eyed Susan, lupine,

Chokecherries

The sour fruit of the large chokecherry shrub is one of the few fruits native to the prairies of eastern Montana.

Native Americans and early settlers harvested these hanging clusters of dark fruit rich in vitamin C. Plains Indians ground up chokecherries and mixed them with dried buffalo meat to form pemmican, which was then eaten, cooked in a soup, or preserved. Cakes of dried chokecherries were a valuable food source in winter.

The chokecherry plant had other uses, too. According to diaries from the Lewis and Clark Expedition, a tea made from the shrub's bark and twigs brought quick relief from stomachaches and diarrhea. Plains tribes used chokecherry wood to make bows and arrows and as fuel for campfires. Chokecherry wood was prized for producing little smoke. ■

sweet clover, aster, shooting stars, violets, and goldenrod. Western Montana also has crocus, fireweed, Oregon grape, and bitterroot.

Serviceberry, buffalo berry, and chokecherry grow along the river valleys. More than 2,000 species of wildflowers and other plants flourish in Montana.

Wildlife

Montana's abundant wildlife includes the grizzly bear, Rocky Mountain goat, bighorn sheep, and moose. These animals prefer remote mountainous areas. More common

Bighorn sheep are among the wildlife native to Montana.

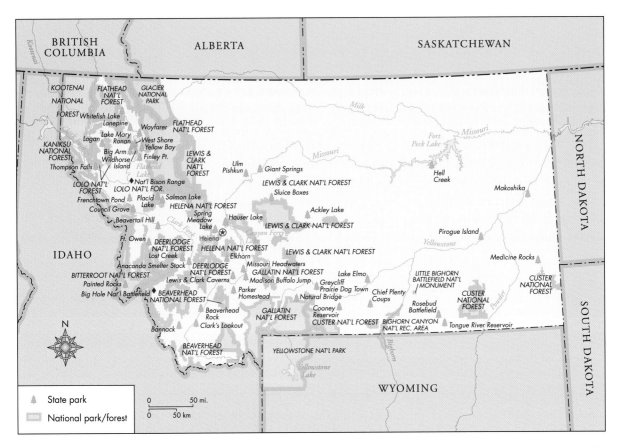

Montana's parks and forests

animals range through much of western Montana. These include big-game animals such as American elk, mule deer, black bear, mountain lion, and bobcat, and smaller animals such as beaver, mink, wolf, squirrel, chipmunk, porcupine, and muskrat.

The eastern plains are home to large populations of pronghorn, mule deer, coyotes, badgers, prairie dogs, and other small mammals. Bison, once numbering in the millions, are found only in the National Bison Range in Flathead Valley and other protected areas.

Montana has about 380 species of birds. Birds of prey include bald eagles, ospreys, and hawks. Game birds include geese, pheas-

Geese in flight

ants, partridges, plains grouse, and wild ducks. The Red Rock Lakes National Wildlife Refuge is home to one of the last remaining populations of trumpeter swans. Hundreds of trumpeter swans also live in Montana's Red Rock Lakes in the southwest corner of the state. Some of the largest waterfowl in North America, adult trumpeter swans can weigh as much as 30 pounds (14 kilograms) and have a wingspan of 8 feet (2 m). Smaller birds such as robins, wrens, hummingbirds, chickadees, magpies, orioles, meadowlarks, blackbirds, swallows, and sparrows are also common in the state.

Montana's streams and lakes swarm with game fish. Some eighty-six species can be found in the state's waters. Cutthroat trout (the state fish), lake trout, rainbow trout, walleye, northern pike, channel catfish, and paddlefish attract local anglers. Kokanee and chinook salmon, perch, brown trout, and Arctic grayling also swim in Montana's waterways.

Montana landscape
blanketed in snow

Climate

Thanks to mild Pacific Ocean breezes, summers are cooler and winters warmer west of the Continental Divide. The eastern slope and plains are affected by Canadian and Arctic air masses in winter and by moisture and heat from the Gulf of Mexico in summer.

East of the Continental Divide, winters are long and harsh. Blizzards strike the state from time to time, but seldom pass westward over the Rocky Mountains. Warm Chinook winds bring the plains some relief from the bitter cold.

Moisture-laden Pacific air masses cool as they move eastward across the Rocky Mountains, causing rain and heavy snowfall. Once air passes the Rocky Mountains, however, it becomes warmer. Rushing down the eastern slope, it warms enough to melt snowdrifts within hours. American Indians called these chinook winds "snow eaters."

Drastic changes in the weather are not unfamiliar to Montanans. One of the fastest changes in temperature occurred in Great Falls on January 11, 1980. In only seven minutes, the temperature rose from –32° Fahrenheit (–36° Celsius) to 15°F (–9°C)— a change of 47°F (27°C).

Montana also holds the world record for a twenty-four-hour temperature change—exactly 100°F (38°C). From January 23, 1916, to January 24, 1916, the temperature in Browning went from 44°F (7°C) to –56°F (–49°C).

Enjoying a warm day in Glacier National Park

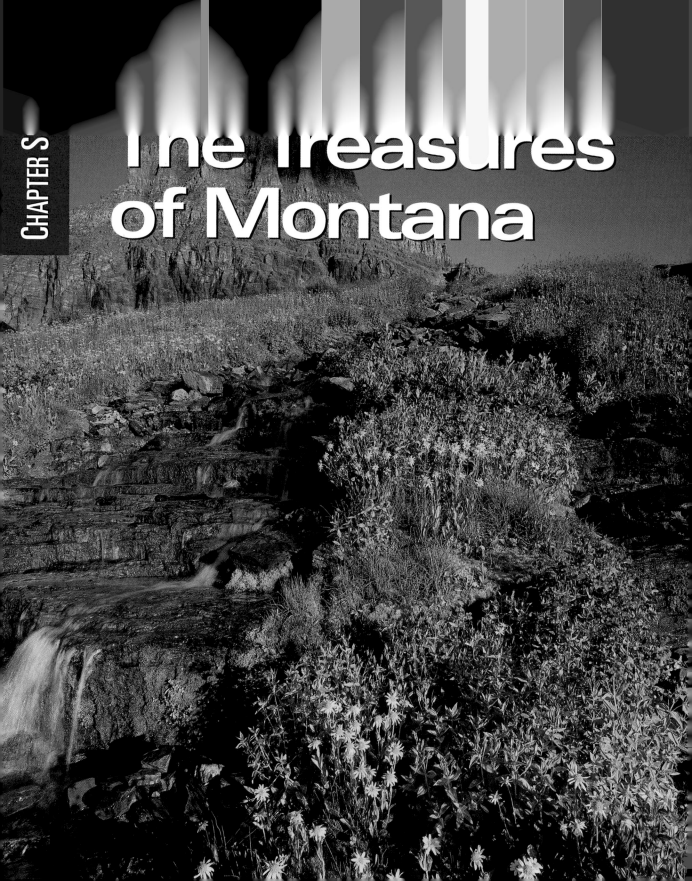

The Treasures of Montana

Going-to-the-Sun Highway

One of the many guidebooks on Montana says, "Montana has never made much sense as one state." In fact, from east to west, Montana has dramatic physical, economic, political, and social differences.

Western Montana, an extension of the Pacific Northwest, enjoys ample rainfall, abundant natural resources, and a diversified economy, and it hosts a majority of the state's population. Eastern Montana, heart of the northern Great Plains, is sparsely populated, semiarid, and more closely associated with the Dakotas than with western Montana. Citizens in northern Montana are likely to travel to the Canadian cities of Regina, Moose Jaw, and Lethbridge for shopping and entertainment.

Opposite: Logan Pass

Glacier Country

An area of striking beauty and subtle contrasts stretches south from Glacier National Park and the Blackfeet Indian Reservation to where the Continental Divide joins the Montana–Idaho border at Lost Trail and Chief Joseph Passes. In addition to the pristine beauty of the state's largest wilderness area, the West's largest natural lake, and Glacier National Park, this region is home to Missoula, western Montana's largest city.

Glacier National Park forms the undisputed centerpiece of the northern Rocky Mountains. Held sacred by the Blackfeet Indians, the sheer scope of this area inspires awe and humility. The magnificent Going-to-the-Sun Highway, completed in 1933 after twenty years of construction, is a 52-mile (84-km) scenic drive. The highway carries visitors from Lake McDonald up 3,000 feet (915 m) to the windswept summit at Logan Pass on the Continental Divide.

Adjacent to the park is the Blackfeet Indian Reservation, home to about 7,000 members of the tribe. In Browning, headquarters for the Blackfeet, the Museum of the Plains Indian has a comprehensive collection of Native American artifacts.

Just south of Glacier National Park lies one of the oldest, largest, and best-known wilderness areas in the nation, the Bob Marshall Wilderness Area. Known affectionately as "the Bob," this 2,400-square-mile (6,216-sq-km) area is named for a young forester from New York whose love of Montana's wilderness sparked the preservation movement of the 1950s.

West of the Bob and south of the town of Kalispell is Flathead Lake, the largest natural freshwater lake in the western United

States. Stretching nearly 30 miles (48 km) along a glacier-dug trench, Flathead Lake is famous for deep-water fishing—deeper than 300 feet (92 m) in places—and for the hundreds of acres of cherry orchards on its eastern shore.

Another attraction on the lake is sprawling Wild Horse Island, once used by Flathead and Kutenai Indians to hide horses from Blackfeet horse-raiding parties. Until a few years ago, the island was home to herds of wild horses. Today it is a state park, a refuge for bald eagles and almost 100 bighorn sheep.

Fog over the Bob Marshall Wilderness Area

The National Bison Range is located near Flathead Lake.

The southern half of the lake is surrounded by the Flathead Indian Reservation, home of the Confederated Flathead and Kutenai tribes. Some 3,700 tribal members living on or near the reservation host several annual powwows, including the Buffalo Feast and Powwow in May, the Standing Arrow Powwow in July, and the War Dance Competition in October.

At the southern end of the reservation is the National Bison Range, established in 1908. Descendants of the millions of American bison that once roamed the Great Plains graze peacefully alongside pronghorn, elk, deer, and bighorn sheep.

Missoula and Hamilton

Farther south is Missoula, Montana's third-largest city. Missoula is home to the University of Montana and considered the state's cultural center. Located at the head of five scenic valleys and the junction of three rivers, Missoula has much to offer. Dozens of museums, gardens, art galleries, and theaters await visitors in what national magazines have called "one of the most sophisticated small cities in America."

Still farther south, in the heart of the Bitterroot Valley, stands the town of Hamilton and the Marcus Daly Mansion called Riverside. Built in 1897 as a summer home, Riverside was enlarged in 1910 to forty-two rooms, including twenty-four bedrooms and fifteen baths. Daly, one of Montana's Copper Kings, made his fortune with the legendary Anaconda Mine.

Montana's cities and interstates

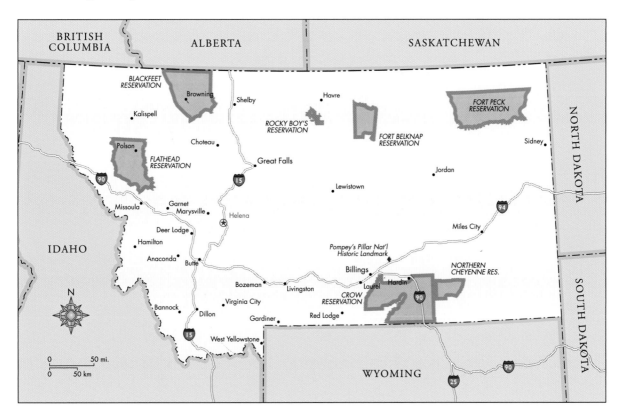

Gold West Country

Montana's southwest corner offers a wealth of history and a history of wealth. Gold, silver, and copper mines brought immigrants to the region from around the world, creating a truly multicultural society. Today, beautiful scenery, bustling cities, abandoned ghost towns, and numerous historical attractions welcome visitors.

Just east of Chief Joseph Pass is Big Hole National Battlefield, site of the 1877 battle between Colonel John Gibbon's troops and five bands of Nez Perce Indians that were fleeing reservation life. Hiking trails, and a visitor center that displays artifacts, tell the tale of this famous battle.

Big Hole National Battlefield

To the northeast lies Anaconda, built in 1883 by Marcus Daly to provide smelting operations for his copper mines. This small town almost beat Helena for the title of state capital. Daly originally called the town Copperopolis, but he renamed after he learned Montana already had a community by the same name, in honor of his copper mine in Butte.

Butte

Butte, once known as "the richest hill on earth," lies to the southeast. The nation's largest single source of silver in the late 1800s, and of copper until the 1930s, Butte was once Montana's largest city, with an estimated 20,000 miners and 100,000 residents. The Butte area became a magnet for immigrants in search of work in the mines.

Foreign-born workers settled in ethnic neighborhoods named Corktown, Dublin Gulch, Finntown, Meaderville, and Chinatown. More than any other city or town in Montana, this largely blue-collar industrial city retains its mixed ethnic character. Due to the dominance of Irish immigrants, the Saint Patrick's Day celebrations in Butte draw thousands.

Recalling the city's mining past, the Copper King Mansion, a three-story, thirty-four-room house built in 1888 by Copper King and politician William A. Clark, is the only privately owned mansion in the state that is open to the public. Tiffany windows, inlaid floors, carved staircases, and a 62-foot (19-m) ballroom adorn

The town of Anaconda

Copper King Mansion

this well-preserved mansion built by Clark when he was one of the world's richest men.

Near the campus of Montana College of Mineral Science and Technology (Montana Tech) is the World Museum of Mining. Sitting on an 1899 mining claim called the Orphan Girl, it includes restored mining structures and equipment, including Hell Roarin' Gulch, a replica of a 1900 mining camp.

Helena

Northeast of Butte is the state capital, Helena. Once a meager prospectors' camp, the bustling city straddles the location of an 1864 gold strike made by four discouraged prospectors on a spot they called their "last chance." The city's main street, called Last Chance Gulch, pays tribute to the strike that touched off a boom era. By 1888, Helena had been transformed from a camp of miners' tents and crude cabins to a city with more millionaires than any other U.S. city its size.

Helena is the capital of Montana.

Today, visitors see historically important structures, such as the original Governor's Mansion, built in the Queen Anne style in 1888, and the elegant state capitol. Domed with Butte copper and containing some of Western artist Charles M. Russell's most acclaimed paintings, this structure was built in 1899 and enlarged in 1912.

Other attractions in this Queen City of the Rockies include the inspiring Cathedral of St. Helena and the Myrna Loy Center for the Performing Arts. Reeder's Alley, a carefully restored part of early-day Helena, features numerous small 1870s-era shanties that now house shops and restaurants.

Ghost Towns

Scattered throughout the southwestern corner of the state are the few remaining ghost towns once populated by gold and silver prospectors and miners. At one time, 600 of these mining camps thrived, but today only about a dozen remain. Bannack, once called

Virginia City was once a busy mining town.

"the toughest town in the West," was the site of Montana's first gold strike in 1862 and served as Montana Territory's first capital. Virginia City and nearby Nevada City sprang up when a major strike on Alder Gulch brought thousands of fortune seekers. Other ghost towns in the area include Garnet, Marysville, and Coolidge.

Russell Country

North-central Montana, immortalized by cowboy artist Charles M. Russell, offers vast open spaces, quiet history, and a glimpse at the prehistoric past. This agricultural region is home to descendants of immigrant farmers, ranchers, and railroad workers, and three Native American tribes that live on two reservations—Rocky Boy and Fort Belknap.

Rocky Boy is home to about 2,500 members of the Chippewa and Cree tribes. The reservation was named in honor of Chippewa leader Stone Child but the name was mistranslated from Chippewa to English as Rocky Boy. The tribes' annual powwow is held in early August.

Members of the Assiniboine and Atsina tribes live on Fort Belknap Indian Reservation. The 4,000 tribal members host several annual events, including a midwinter fair in February, Milk River Indian Days in late July, and the Christmas Powwow.

Giant Springs State Park

Great Falls

The state's second-largest city, Great Falls, offers a variety of attractions. Located among five waterfalls that create a formidable barrier for travelers on the Missouri River, this area was an important stop for Lewis and Clark in 1805. The Lewis and Clark National Historic Trail Interpretive Center contains exhibits focusing on the interaction between Lewis and Clark and the Native Americans the explorers encountered along the way.

One geographic feature that caught the attention of Lewis and Clark was a gushing natural spring, now called Giant Springs. This spring still flows into the Missouri River in the northeast corner of Great Falls. The mineral-rich water flows from the spring via the world's shortest river—the Roe.

Another museum, one of the state's finest, is the C. M. Russell Museum. It houses one of the world's most complete collections of Russell's original art and personal items, including his log-cabin studio and house.

Choteau

West of Great Falls, the small town of Choteau is well known to the world's paleontologists as a result of discoveries in the area. Scientists from around the world come to investigate the former dinosaur-breeding ground. Egg Mountain, just west of town, made

Paleontologists in Montana

In 1902, the American Museum of Natural History sent Dr. Barnum Brown to the area around Jordan, Montana, in search of dinosaur remains. Brown's party, searching the eroded bluffs along Hell Creek, uncovered an amazing find—two fossilized skeletons of *Tyrannosaurus rex*. Since that time, the Hell Creek Formation has yielded seven T-Rex skeletons, along with specimens of the triceratops, duck-billed dinosaur and *Mosasaurus*, dinosaur eggs, and other petrified animal remains.

Dr. John R. "Jack" Horner, born in Shelby, discovered the first dinosaur nests near Choteau. Beliefs about dinosaurs changed radically thanks to this discovery, which indicated that the huge reptiles were possibly related to birds. Horner has received major research grants from the National Science Foundation and the MacArthur Foundation, and he serves as curator of paleontology for the Museum of the Rockies in Bozeman. He also served as an adviser on Steven Spielberg's film *Jurassic Park*. ■

paleontological history in the 1970s when the site yielded not only adult dinosaur skeletons but also the bones of juvenile dinosaurs and nests of fossilized eggs. These discoveries, made by Jack Horner, revolutionized scientific theories about dinosaurs, which are now thought to be closely related to birds.

Yellowstone Country

The area around Bozeman in south-central Montana is truly Yellowstone Country. America's first national park is just to the south, and its longest free-flowing river—the Yellowstone—gives the region its nickname. Visitors enjoy wilderness scenery in Yellow-

The Yellowstone River Valley

stone National Park and along Beartooth Highway, one of North America's most scenic drives. Cultural and historical attractions draw visitors to Bozeman and Red Lodge.

Three of the entrances to Yellowstone National Park lie in Montana. The west entrance, in West Yellowstone, Montana, is a year-round outdoor recreation center. Known as the Snowmobile Capital of the World, West Yellowstone offers hundreds of miles of snowmobile trails, cross-country ski trails, and excellent fly-fishing.

The northern entrance to Yellowstone, near Gardiner, was dedicated by President Theodore Roosevelt in 1903 and is still the only park entrance open to automobile traffic year-round. Visitors take a boardwalk to the terraced hot pools at Mammoth Hot Springs.

Beartooth Highway cuts through the Beartooth Mountains.

Beartooth Highway

To arrive at the northeast entrance to Yellowstone, visitors might literally take a trip through the clouds. The famous Beartooth Highway, beginning in Red Lodge, climbs up glacier-carved walls by way of switchbacks and hairpin turns until it reaches an elevation of 10,947 feet (3,339 m).

CBS correspondent Charles Kuralt called Beartooth "the most beautiful roadway in America." The 68-mile (109-km) road has been designated a national scenic byway. From the summit, called the Top of the World, a panoramic view of snow-capped peaks and plateaus, alpine lakes, and the ski lift leaves visitors breathless.

Red Lodge

Some say Red Lodge, founded as a coal-mining camp, gets its name from Crow Indians who decorated their lodges with red clay. Many European immigrants later came to the area to work in the mines. Each year in early August, the town hosts a nine-day Festival of Nations honoring its ethnic and cultural origins.

During the celebration, each ethnic group celebrates on a different day. Scandinavian, Scottish, German, Finnish, Yugoslavian, English, Irish, and Italian Days are followed by Montana Day and All Nations Day. International foods, traditional dances, folk-art displays, and parades mark the event.

Bozeman

Bozeman is named for an early explorer and guide named John Bozeman. The city has a small-town atmosphere but offers art galleries, museums, a symphony orchestra, opera, and the world's second museum devoted entirely to the history of the computer.

The Festival of Nations is held each year in Red Lodge.

Located at the base of the Bridger Range, Bozeman is the home of Montana State University. At the Museum of the Rockies, visitors can review 4 billion years of the history of the northern Rocky Mountains. Museum treasures include the Taylor Planetarium; extensive displays of dinosaur skeletons, including a *Tyrannosaurus rex* skull unearthed in eastern Montana in 1990; and Native American and early pioneer artifacts.

A dinosaur exhibit at the Museum of the Rockies

Missouri River Country

The northeast corner of Montana is a wildlife-lover's dream. Millions of migratory waterfowl fill the sky above the region's many lakes and reservoirs during peak migration seasons. Fort Peck Lake, the state's largest man-made lake, offers excellent fishing for northern pike, walleye, paddlefish, and lake trout. The Charles M. Russell National Wildlife Refuge surrounds the lake, providing sanctuary for millions of animals.

Many visitors come to northeastern Montana to study the region's history and prehistory. Fossil hunters flock to the Hell Creek area, north of Jordan.

History buffs travel to Fort Union and the Fort Peck Indian Reservation. Originally built as an Indian trading post, Fort Union

The Charles M. Russell National Wildlife Refuge

Nearly 1.1 million acres (445,500 ha) of isolated, forbidding terrain in east-central Montana have been set aside as sanctuary for some 200 species of birds, 45 species of mammals, and countless reptiles and fish. The refuge, surrounding Fort Peck Lake, is home to large numbers of mule deer, pronghorn, sage grouse, prairie dogs, and mountain plovers. Elk and bighorn sheep also live here year-round.

The refuge is named for famed cowboy artist Charles M. Russell, whose paintings often depicted the rugged beauty of the bluffs and canyons along the Missouri River. Established in 1936, the CMR, as it is known locally, is the second-largest wildlife refuge outside of Alaska. ▪

served as an important fur-trading post from the 1820s to the 1860s. Today, this reconstructed frontier outpost hosts the annual Fort Union Rendezvous each summer. The Rendezvous re-creates the days when trappers and traders gathered to swap stories and compete in hatchet-throwing and black-powder-rifle shooting contests.

Fort Peck Indian Reservation is home to about 6,800 members of the Assiniboine and Dakota peoples. It is bordered on the south by the Missouri River. Annual celebrations at Fort Peck include the Red Bottom Celebration in mid-June, the Badlands Celebration a week later, the Fort Kipp and Iron Ring Celebrations and Wild Horse Stampede in July, and Poplar Indian Days Celebration in September.

Billings

Billings, the state's largest city, is located in the northeast corner of Montana. A large sales and trade center, Billings is at the heart of

The Billings skyline
at night

a vast agricultural region that extends into nearby states and into Canada's prairie provinces. Home to two universities—Rocky Mountain College and Montana State University at Billings—the city offers museums, art galleries, and theaters.

Just northeast of Billings along the Yellowstone River lies Pompey's Pillar National Historic Landmark. Captain William A. Clark carved his name on a sandstone butte there in 1806. This graffiti is the only remaining physical evidence of the explorers along the trail followed by the Lewis and Clark Expedition.

Indian Reservations

Southeast of Billings lies the Crow Reservation. Every August, the Crow Fair and Rodeo Celebration, one of the largest Native American powwows in North America, takes place here. Competitive native dances, wild-horse races, parades, games of skill and chance, and family reunions draw thousands of visitors each year.

In the remote southeast corner of the reservation, the Bighorn River was dammed in 1965, creating Bighorn Lake. Because

Crow hold the lands in Bighorn Canyon and the Pryor and Bighorn Mountains sacred, the tribe decided to restrict the area to Native Americans. The state of Montana then took the Crow to court to reopen public access to the river. The case was known as the Battle of the Bighorn. The Supreme Court ruled in favor of the state in 1981, and the Bighorn is now one of the best fishing spots in America.

The Crow Reservation is also the site of the Little Bighorn Battlefield National Monument, where Dakota, Cheyenne, and Arapaho warriors overwhelmed George Armstrong Custer's forces.

A reenactment of the Battle of Little Bighorn

Each June, citizens of Hardin, just northwest of the site, stage a reenactment of the famous battle.

East of the Crow Reservation is the Northern Cheyenne Indian Reservation, home to 5,000 Northern Cheyenne and members of various other tribes. Each January, they host a powwow, followed in May with the Northern Cheyenne Powwow and Rodeo. In early July, the reservation town of Lame Deer hosts another Northern Cheyenne Powwow. In late December, the town of Busby hosts the Christmas Powwow.

CHAPTER SEVEN

Progressive Montana

n 1972, delegates to Montana's third constitutional convention drew up a 12,000-word document to replace the state's 1889 constitution. The new document is considered one of the most progressive state constitutions in America. It contains a revised bill of rights that adds to the traditional rights of free speech, religion, press, and assembly. It stipulates the right to a clean and healthful environment, the right to participate in governmental decision making, the right of individual privacy, and the right to know about and participate in public processes. In addition, it declares that all water within the state, even on private land, is under state control.

A mural by Charles Russell adorns one wall in the chambers of Montana's house of representatives.

The 1972 document streamlined state government and combined more than 100 agencies into 15 departments that answer directly to the governor. A state referendum is required every twenty years to vote on another constitutional convention. Montana's state constitution is also the only one in America with a stated commitment to preserve the "cultural integrity" of its Native American tribes.

Amendments to the 1972 state constitution may be proposed by a two-thirds vote of state legislators, a petition, or constitutional convention. Two-thirds of the legislators and a majority of voters must approve amendments proposed by the legislature. Amend-

Opposite: The state capitol in Helena

Inside the capitol

ments proposed by popular petition, if signed by at least 10 percent of the electorate in two-fifths of the state's legislative districts, require only a simple majority of the state's voters to be approved.

Montana's state government consists of an executive branch, a legislative branch, and a judicial branch. The executive branch takes care of the state's day-to-day operations. The legislative branch proposes and passes laws governing the state. The judicial branch—the state's courts—interprets and reviews laws and tries civil and criminal cases.

Executive Branch

The executive branch consists of the governor, lieutenant governor, secretary of state, attorney general, auditor, superintendent of public instruction, and five public-service commissioners. Each of these officials is publicly elected and serves a four-year term. Managed by these individuals are numerous state agencies, which are assigned the daily duties of state operations.

The governor's duties are partly ceremonial, partly advisory, and partly administrative. As chief executive officer of the state, he or she makes sure that all state laws are properly executed. As commander in chief of the state militia, the governor may call out troops to protect public safety and property in the event of a

Montana's Governors

Name	Party	Term	Name	Party	Term
Joseph K. Toole	Dem.	1889–1893	Sam C. Ford	Rep.	1941–1949
John E. Rickards	Rep.	1893–1897	John W. Bonner	Dem.	1949–1953
Robert B. Smith	Dem.-Pop.	1897–1901	J. Hugo Aronson	Rep.	1953–1961
Joseph K. Toole	Dem.	1901–1908	Donald G. Nutter	Rep.	1961–1962
Edwin L. Norris	Dem.	1908–1913	Tim M. Babcock	Rep.	1962–1969
S. V. Stewart	Dem.	1913–1921	Forrest H. Anderson	Dem.	1969–1973
Joseph M. Dixon	Rep.	1921–1925	Thomas L. Judge	Dem.	1973–1981
John E. Erickson	Dem.	1925–1933	Ted Schwinden	Dem.	1981–1989
Frank H. Cooney	Dem.	1933–1935	Stan Stephens	Rep.	1989–1993
W. Elmer Holt	Dem.	1935–1937	Marc Racicot	Rep.	1993–
Roy E. Ayers	Dem.	1937–1941			

natural disaster or insurrection (rebellion). The governor also acts as Montana's spokesperson, working with other states and the federal government.

As ceremonial head of state, the governor welcomes official visitors and dedicates public buildings. Duties of the governor also include appointing certain state officials, with legislative

Marc Racicot (1948–)

Montana's twentieth governor, Marc Racicot, traces his roots within the state all the way back to the 1860s, when his grandfather worked as a logging-camp cook in northwestern Montana.

Racicot was born in Thompson Falls. He starred on the basketball team and was elected student-body president at Carroll College in Helena. Then he earned his law degree from the University of Montana Law School in 1973.

After three years in the army, Racicot returned to Montana and became deputy county attorney for Missoula County. He became attorney general in 1988. Racicot, a member of the Republican Party, won a close race for governor in 1992 and a landslide reelection victory in 1996. ■

approval. The governor may approve or veto laws passed by the leg-islature. He or she has the privilege of item veto, which means that specific parts of a proposal can be vetoed without rejecting the entire bill.

The governor's assistant in the executive branch is the lieutenant governor. He or she steps in whenever the governor is unable to complete duties, because of death, resignation, or incapacity. The lieutenant governor also serves as acting governor at the written

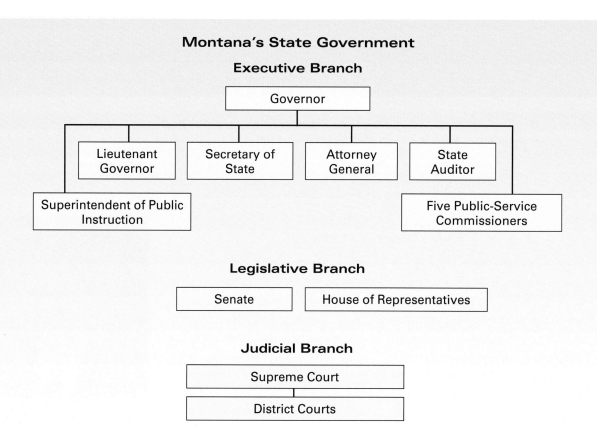

Montana's State Government

Executive Branch

Governor

Lieutenant Governor

Secretary of State

Attorney General

State Auditor

Superintendent of Public Instruction

Five Public-Service Commissioners

Legislative Branch

Senate

House of Representatives

Judicial Branch

Supreme Court

District Courts

request of the governor or if the governor has been out of the state for more than forty-five consecutive days.

The secretary of state keeps official state records and is in charge of state elections. The attorney general is the state's chief legal officer, serving as prosecutor or defense attorney in cases involving the state.

The state auditor oversees financial operations. The superintendent of public instruction regulates the schools. The Montana Public Service Commission regulates the state's public utilities.

Legislative Branch

The Montana legislature has a house of representatives and a senate. The 1972 constitution requires the house to have at least 80 but no more than 100 members and the senate to have no fewer than 40 but not more than 50 members.

Jeannette Rankin (1880–1973)

Jeannette Rankin, born in Missoula, attended the University of Montana. In 1914, she campaigned for women's suffrage—the right to vote. In 1916, she was elected to the U.S. Congress, becoming the first woman elected to national office in the United States.

Rankin was opposed to the United States's entering World War I. She lost her seat in the next election, but in 1940, she was elected to the U.S. House of Representatives. When Congress voted on a declaration of war against Japan in 1941, Rankin was the only member to vote against it. "As a woman I cannot go to war, and I refuse to send anybody else," she declared.

She left Congress after her term expired, but she never stopped standing up for her principles. In 1968, at the age of eighty-eight, she led a group of women in a march on Washington, D.C., to protest the Vietnam War. ■

Representatives are elected for two-year terms from 100 house districts. Every two years, half the senators are elected to serve four-year terms. Representatives are limited to no more than four terms, and senators serve no more than two.

The legislature meets in odd-numbered years for a term of ninety days. Sessions begin on the first Monday in January. Special sessions can be called by the governor or by written request from a majority of legislators.

Judicial Branch

Montana has a three-tiered court structure. The highest level, the Montana Supreme Court, is made up of seven members—the chief justice and six associate justices. Each is elected to an eight-year term in public elections, without party designations.

The primary duty of the state supreme court is to review rulings of the state's lower courts and decide appeals from the district

Montana's Capitol

Construction on the capitol, designed by Charles Emlen Bell and John Hackett Kent, began on Independence Day, 1899. The building was dedicated on July 4, 1902. The structure, faced in sandstone from Columbus, Montana, cost about $485,000 and sits on donated land.

Ten years after its dedication, an expansion project added East and West Wings faced with Jefferson County granite. The capitol rotunda is built in the French Renaissance style with Ionic columns. The rotunda has a terrazzo tile floor and four frescoes representing a Native American, a cowboy, an explorer-trapper, and a prospector. The rotunda also has a statue of Jeannette Rankin, the first woman ever elected to the U.S. Congress. ■

courts. It also establishes rules governing appeals processes, legal procedure for the lower courts, and state requirements for becoming a lawyer. The court holds four terms, beginning on the first Tuesday of March, June, October, and December. Each year, the Montana Supreme Court hears about 600 cases.

The second tier in Montana's judicial system consists of twenty-one judicial districts and thirty-seven district court judges. These judges, elected by district-wide vote, preside over the state's trial courts for a term of six years, with jurisdiction, or authority, in civil and criminal cases. These judges hear an average of 30,000 cases per year.

The third tier in the court system includes justice of the peace courts, city or municipal courts, and special courts such as workers' compensation court and water court. These courts

The capitol rotunda ceiling has four painted frescoes that represent Montana's history.

Montana's State Flag and Seal

The Montana state flag was originally a banner for the First Territorial Montana Infantry in 1898. The group of volunteers, under the leadership of Colonel Harry C. Kessler, trained at Fort William Henry Harrison, near Helena, for combat in the Spanish-American War (1898). A seamstress commissioned by Kessler embroidered the state seal on a dark blue background. The 1905 legislative assembly honored the First Montana Infantry by voting to use an exact rendition of their banner as the state's official flag. The word MONTANA in bold yellow letters was added above the state seal in 1981.

Commissioning the design of the official seal of Montana was one of the first acts of the territorial government in 1865. The central image consists of a miner's pick and shovel and a plow. These items, representing major economic interests in the state, are surrounded by the image of the Great Falls of the Missouri River on the right and a mountain scene on the left. Below these images is a banner with the state's motto, *Oro y Plata* (Gold and Silver). On March 2, 1893, Governor J. E. Rickards signed the document proclaiming the design the state's official seal. ■

Montana's State Symbols

State flower: Bitterroot In 1895, the bitterroot (left) with its pink daisylike blossoms became the first state symbol chosen for Montana. Bitterroot grows on mountain slopes in western Montana and blooms in late spring and early summer.

State tree: Ponderosa pine Standing from 60 to 200 feet (18 to 61 m) tall at maturity (150 years), the ponderosa pine was officially designated Montana's state tree in 1949 after a year-long campaign by the Montana Federation of Garden Clubs.

State bird: Western meadowlark This brown speckled bird has a bright yellow vest and a black V-shaped necklace. Montana's schoolchildren chose the western meadowlark as the state bird in 1930. The state legislature made it official the following year.

State mammal: Grizzly bear Montana's schoolchildren chose the grizzly bear (above) as the state mammal in 1982. Only about 1,000 grizzlies live in the American West today. They once numbered as many as 50,000 and ranged as far east as the Mississippi River. Federally protected by the Endangered Species Act, these animals weigh up to 800 pounds (363 kg) and rise on their hind legs to a height of 12 feet (3.7 m).

State fish: Blackspotted cutthroat trout The cutthroat is so named because of a red slash under its jaw. Once abundant in Montana rivers, the blackspotted cutthroat trout has been overfished in many areas. It is now considered a sensitive species by the USDA Forest Service.

State gemstones: Sapphire and moss agate The 1969 state legislature chose two stones to represent Montana. Since 1896, deep blue sapphires have been mined along Yogo Creek, southwest of Utica, in the central part of the state. Moss agates are easily found along the Yellowstone River. A form of quartz, agate may be yellow, orange, brown, or black, and is used for jewelry.

State fossil: Duck-billed dinosaur Middle-school students presented 8,000 petition signatures to the state legislature in 1985 asking that the duck-billed dinosaur be named the state fossil. Numerous examples of this prehistoric beast have been unearthed at Egg Mountain, near Choteau, site of the world's largest-known accumulation of dinosaur fossils. They grew to 30 feet (9.2 m) in length and weighed 3 tons.

State grass: Bluebunch wheatgrass This grass is an important food source for cattle and sheep.

Montana's State Song
"Montana"

Music by Joseph E. Howard
Words by Charles C. Cohen
"Montana" was designated the state song in 1945.

Tell me of that Treasure State
Story always new,
Tell of its beauties grand
And its hearts so true.

Mountains of sunset fire
The land I love the best
Let me grasp the hand of one
From out the Golden West.

Chorus:
Montana, Montana,
Glory of the West
Of all the states from coast to
coast,
You're easily the best.
Montana, Montana,
Where skies are always blue
M-O-N-T-A-N-A,
Montana, I love you.

Each country has its flow'r;
Each one plays a part,
Each bloom brings a longing
hope
To some lonely heart.

Bitterroot to me is dear
Growing in my land
Sing then that glorious air
The one I understand.

(Chorus)

handle smaller cases, and judges are elected in local county or city elections.

Local Government

The 1972 state constitution, which took effect in 1973, required all cities, towns, and counties to set up committees to review local government and suggest alternatives. Of the fifty-six counties in Montana, fifty-three elect three county commissioners who serve six-year terms. These commissioners exercise legislative, executive, and administrative powers.

County governments are responsible for local elections, collection of local taxes, official record keeping, maintenance of

Montana's counties

roads and bridges, and law enforcement. Municipalities have police forces and other local agencies to deal with day-to-day issues. About 120 of Montana's cities have mayor-council types of government. Helena, Bozeman, and Great Falls use the council-manager system.

Tribal Governments

Eleven Native American tribes occupy seven reservations in Montana. Southwest of Glacier National Park, the Flathead Reservation is home to the Flathead, the Kutenai, and the Pend d'Oreille. East of the park is the Blackfeet Indian Reservation. North-central

Residents of Montana's Native American reservations observe tribal laws.

Montana is the site of Rocky Boy, home of the Chippewa and the Cree, and Fort Belknap, where the Assiniboine and the Atsina live. In the far northeastern corner of the state, the Fort Peck Reservation has Assiniboine and Dakota residents. Along Montana's border with Wyoming are the Crow and Northern Cheyenne Reservations.

Although not all reservation land is owned by Native Americans, tribal law prevails within reservation boundaries. Independent political units run the schools, regulate trade, levy local taxes, conduct elections, maintain intergovernmental relations with federal, state, and local authorities, write constitutions, and enforce laws.

State Revenues

Almost one-third of Montana's revenues come from federal grants. One-half comes from taxes. Tax revenue in the state comes from individual income taxes, coal-production taxes, taxes on motor fuels and tobacco, property taxes, and corporate income taxes. Principal expenditures go to education, public welfare, and highways.

National Politics

In Montana's early statehood, the Democratic Party dominated because many of the state's citizens had come from the South, fleeing the Civil War and its aftermath. During the twentieth century, Democrats and Republicans more or less shared power. In national elections since 1952, the state has voted for the Republican presidential candidates in every election—except in 1964, when it voted for Lyndon B. Johnson, and in 1992, when it voted for Bill Clinton.

Since the 1990 U.S. census, Montana has had only one representative in the House of Representatives, making it the largest and most populous congressional district in the country. Montana has two U.S. senators.

CHAPTER EIGHT

Montana at Work

Montana's economy has gone through many changes since statehood. The fur trade flourished in the early to mid-1800s. After the gold strikes of the 1860s, mining for gold, silver, and eventually copper and zinc dominated. The huge influx of miners and prospectors and the removal of Native Americans from the Plains in the 1870s encouraged ranching.

Early settlements in Montana were farming communities.

Farming began in the early 1900s when officials of the Great Northern Railway lured waves of homesteaders to the area. They established settlements along the Hi-Line, the railroad built in the 1880s to connect the northern plains to the Rocky Mountains and eastern markets. These mostly European immigrants, believing the pamphlets they had received when they stepped off ships on the East Coast, expected fertile soil, abundant rainfall, and 320 acres (130 ha) of free land per person.

The severe drought that began in 1917 caused many newly established farms to be abandoned. Improvements in irrigation and dryland farming techniques after the 1930s led to significant recovery in agriculture, however. The 1950s brought the petroleum and natural-gas industries to eastern Montana, and the 1970s brought an increase in coal mining. Amid all these

Opposite: Harvesting wheat

**A ranch hand shoeing
a horse**

changes in the state's economic focus, tourism and service industries increased steadily.

Montana's economy depends on natural resources. The manufacturing industry is almost entirely involved in creating wood products or processing food.

Service Industries

As in most other states, service industries account for the largest percentage of the gross state product (GSP). The GSP is the total value of goods and services that a state produces in a year. Service industries are also by far the largest employer in the state.

Especially important in the state's urban areas, service industries in finance, real estate, and insurance contribute the largest share of Montana's GSP, although they employ only 4 percent of the workforce.

The wholesale and retail trade industry employs the largest number of Montanans. These businesses include the wholesale trade of food products, motor vehicles, and mineral products (such as oil and gas), and retail businesses such as grocery stores, discount and department stores, gas stations, and restaurants.

Following closely behind wholesale and retail trade are community, business, and personal services. These industries, centered primarily in the state's cities, include law firms, doctors' offices and private clinics, hotels and motels, and countless other types of services.

Local, state, and federal governments employ 20 percent of the workforce. State government in Helena, Malmstrom Air Force Base near Great Falls, and national parks, monuments, and wildlife refuges provide numerous jobs.

Transportation

Because of Montana's vast distances, transportation industries are crucial to the state's economy. Trucking firms and railroads transport freight within the state. Good highway and track maintenance is essential. Extremes in weather, such as freezing and thawing, make this job difficult and costly. Montana's transportation system includes almost 70,000 miles (112,630 km) of public roads, but only 25 percent have paved surfaces. Most roadways run east to west, with relatively few north-south routes. The state has about 3,400 miles (5,471 km) of rail lines.

A train passing through the Moccasin Mountains

Air travel centers primarily in Billings and Great Falls. The state has 130 public and 82 private airports. Passenger trains serve ten Montana cities along the Hi-Line.

Communication

Montanans keep up with local, state, and world news through ten major daily newspapers and seventy-five local papers (weekly or semiweekly). The *Billings Gazette*, circulation 60,000, is the state's largest paper, followed by the *Great Falls Tribune* and *The Missoulian*. Radio stations came to Montana in 1922, when KFBB began broadcasting from Great Falls. Approximately 110 radio stations broadcast in the state today. The television age arrived in 1953 with stations KXLF-TV (still in operation) and KOPR-TV in Billings. About twenty commercial TV stations and numerous cable systems keep Montanans connected to the rest of the world. Public-television programming comes from KUSM-TV in Bozeman and KUFM-TV in Missoula.

Mel Ruder (1915–)

Mel Ruder came to Columbia Falls in 1946. He founded the *Hungry Horse News* and served as its editor, publisher, reporter, and photographer. His coverage of the floods in Glacier National Park in June 1964 earned him a Pulitzer Prize for local reporting. The *Hungry Horse News* is the only Montana newspaper to win a Pulitzer. He also won a National Press Award for his newspaper's use of photographs and was given honorary membership in the Blackfeet tribe for Native American news coverage. Ruder retired from the newspaper in 1978. ▩

Public Utilities

Public utilities round out Montana's service industries. Coal-burning plants provide nearly 60 percent of the state's electrical power. Hydroelectric generators supply the other 40 percent. Ranked among the nation's top ten producers of hydroelectric power, Montana plants, including Fort Peck and Canyon Ferry on the Missouri River, Hungry Horse on the South Fork Flathead River, and Noxon Rapids on the Clark Fork, generate billions of kilowatt hours of electric power.

A worker at an electric plant

Minerals and Mining

Gold, silver, and copper mining dominated the state's economy in the nineteenth century. Today, coal and petroleum lead the way. Providing 7 percent of the GSP, the state's mining industry still produces precious metals, but fuel minerals—coal, petroleum, and natural gas—account for almost 80 percent of Montana's income from mineral production.

Subbituminous, or soft, coal lies under much of southeastern Montana. Modern strip-mining techniques unearth millions of tons from surface mines in Big Horn and Rosebud Counties. Estimates of the state's coal reserves are in excess of 50 billion tons.

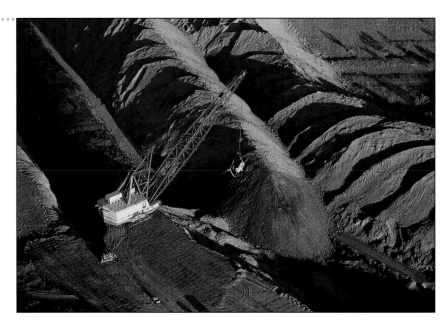

A Montana coal mine

Petroleum production, concentrated in the Elk Basin, Cut Bank, and Williston Basin fields and at Bell Creek near Broadus, began in Montana in the early 1920s. About 1 percent of the nation's petroleum is produced in Montana. Exploration continues, and the potential for expansion is promising. Most of the state's natural gas comes from the Williston Basin, along the North Dakota border.

Gold and copper are Montana's most valuable nonfuel minerals. The state's largest gold mine is located near Whitehall, in Jefferson County. Stillwater County, west of Billings, has the only mine in the nation that produces platinum and palladium.

What Montana Grows, Manufactures, and Mines

Agriculture	Manufacturing	Mining
Barley	Food products	Coal
Beef cattle	Refined petroleum	Copper
Hay	Wood products	Gold
Sheep		Petroleum
Wheat		

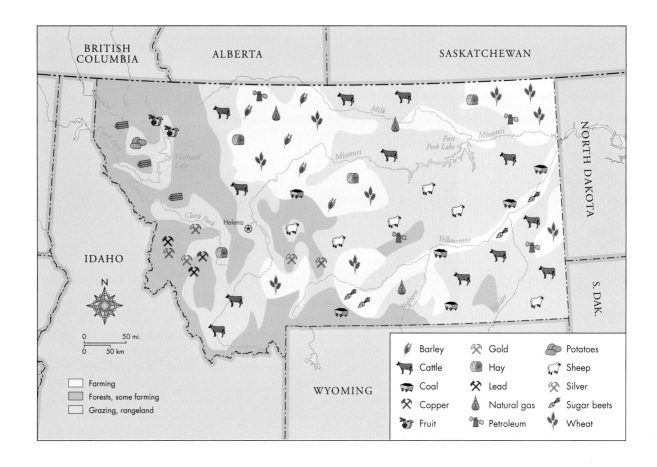

Montana ranks first in the nation in the production of talc; fifth in copper, gold, and zinc; and seventh in the production of gemstones, such as sapphires, garnets, and agates. Southwest of Utica, the area around Yogo Gulch has produced $10 million worth of gem-quality sapphires since 1896.

Completing Montana's list of mined products are antimony from Sanders County, vermiculite from Lincoln County, and phosphate rock from several western counties. The state also produces gypsum, limestone, sand, and gravel. In addition, 80 percent of the known chrome reserves in North America are found in Montana.

The New World Mine Controversy

In the early 1990s, Crown Butte Mine, Inc., proposed opening a huge open-pit gold mine, called the New World Mine, north of Cooke City. Environmental groups, officials from Yellowstone National Park, and President Bill Clinton opposed the project. They felt the mine, which would affect three main watersheds and interfere with grizzly bear migration routes, would be too damaging.

The mining company proposed storing waste from the mine in huge ponds, but critics feared that natural forces such as earthquakes and the resulting landslides could release the highly acidic fluid, resulting in catastrophic damage to the environment.

The controversy ended in 1996 when the federal government purchased mineral rights to the area for $65 million. The company also agreed to pay $22.5 million to help clean up environmental damage. ▧

Lumbering

Forests cover more than 22 million acres (8.9 million ha) in Montana, including more than 14 million acres (5.7 million ha) of commercial timberland. Commercial native species include

Dennis Washington (1935–)

Since 1989, Dennis Washington has been one of the 400 richest Americans, according to *Forbes* magazine. Chairman of the Washington Corporation, the Missoula industrialist won the Horatio Alger Award in 1995 for overcoming the adversity of childhood polio and fighting his way to success. Washington, once the largest contractor in Montana, bought the Anaconda Company copper mine and other Atlantic Richfield holdings in 1986. ■

Douglas fir, larch, ponderosa pine, lodgepole pine, Engelmann spruce, red cedar, Rocky Mountain juniper, and hemlock. From this abundance of timber, the state produces finished lumber, fuel wood, fence posts, plywood, particleboard, Christmas trees, and paper. Log-home manufacturers in Montana lead the nation in home-kit production. Many of these kits are shipped overseas, especially to Japan.

Feeding cattle from a hay wagon

Agriculture

Nearly two-thirds of Montana's land is used for agricultural purposes. Montana's farms and ranches number about 22,000. Farms and ranches average nearly 2,900 acres (1,175 ha), more than five times the national average.

Many people think of Montana as an agricultural state, yet

The Bair Family

Charles M. Bair (1857–1943) came to Montana as a train conductor in 1883. He then established a ranching empire almost unrivaled in the West.

Bair acquired a large ranch in the Musselshell River Valley and he also obtained grazing rights on the nearby Crow Indian Reservation. At one time, his herd (300,000 sheep) was supposedly the largest in North America. The bulk of Charles Bair's fortune, however, was made in the Yukon gold rush.

The Bair financial empire included interests in coal-mining, cattle, oil, banking, and irrigation projects. Bair and his daughters, Marguerite and Alberta, toured Europe many times, collecting priceless antiques and works of art. Their world-renowned collection fills their twenty-six-room Montana ranch house at Martinsdale. Bair's youngest daughter lived there until her death in 1993. In 1996, the home and ranch headquarters became a public museum. ▪

fewer than 10 percent of its people make a living from farming and ranching. Even so, Montana ranks second only to Texas in farm and ranch acreage.

Wheat is the state's chief crop. Spring wheat is grown mostly in central and northeastern Montana, and winter wheat is concentrated in the south. In 1995, wheat provided more than one-third of the state's agricultural income.

Other crops raised in Montana include barley, grown mostly north of Great Falls; oats; corn, grown chiefly for feed; hay, mostly alfalfa; potatoes; Great Northern beans; and sugar beets. Western Montana's milder climate is suitable for fruits and berries, sweet cherries (in the Flathead Lake region), and apples.

Lamb Kebobs

This popular summertime dish from Montana is delicious broiled or grilled.

Ingredients:

- ¼ cup olive oil
- ¼ cup lemon juice
- 1 small garlic clove, minced
- 1 scallion, thinly sliced
- ¼ teaspoon coriander, ground
- ½ teaspoon salt, or to taste
- ½ teaspoon cayenne pepper, if desired
- 1½ pounds leg of lamb, boneless

Directions:

Cut the lamb into 1-inch squares. In a small bowl, combine the olive oil, lemon juice, garlic, scallion, and coriander. Season with salt and cayenne pepper.

Add the lamb to the mixture and marinate for up to three hours at room temperature or six hours in the refrigerator. Be sure to turn the lamb in the marinade a few times.

String the lamb cubes on kebob skewers. Place the skewers on the grill or a pan 4 to 5 inches (10 to 13 cm) under a preheated broiler for 6 to 7 minutes, or until the lamb is cooked through.

Serves 4

Livestock and livestock products—milk, cheese, and eggs—contribute almost half the state's agricultural income. Beef-cattle production provides the largest share. Some of the nation's largest cattle ranches are in Montana's rolling hills and mountain valleys. In 1995, cattle outnumbered people three to one, and the sale of cattle and calves amounted to almost $700 million.

Sheep and hog farms also contribute to Montana's farm economy. Sheep production is concentrated in Garfield and Carter Counties. Hog production is centered in several counties just east of the Rocky Mountains in northwest and north-central Montana. The Hutterite colonies of east-central Montana produce a large percentage of Montana's market hogs.

Sheep are among the the types of livestock raised in Montana.

Manufacturing

Slow to develop in the state, manufacturing provides only 7 percent of the GSP and employs only 6 percent of the workforce. The state's distance from major markets, the high cost of transportation, and the small labor force restrict the profits from manufacturing.

Manufacturing is limited to processing raw materials. The world's largest lead smelter is in East Helena. Great Falls, Billings, Cut Bank, and Laurel have oil refineries.

Logs waiting for processing outside a sawmill

Four large sawmills—at Bonner, Columbia Falls, Kalispell, and Libby—and seventy smaller mills process much of western Montana's timber into wood products that are eventually transformed into mining timbers, pencils, prefabricated homes, telephone poles, plywood, and fence posts.

Other manufactured products include aluminum, printed materials, paper products, concrete, and refined petroleum. Food processing, centered mostly in Billings and Great Falls, involves meatpacking, soft-drink bottling, milk processing, and grain milling. The value added by manufacture (that is, the difference in value from raw materials to finished product) of Montana's manufactured goods is $1.75 billion per year.

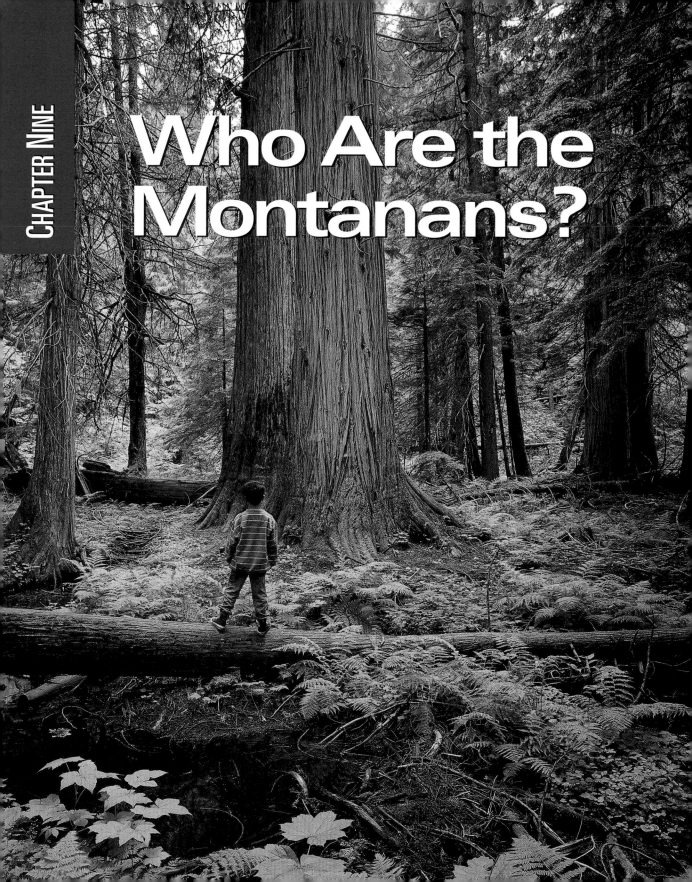

CHAPTER NINE

Who Are the Montanans?

A merica's Outback is the nickname for the upper Great Plains and northern Rocky Mountains. In the last state to be settled by white pioneers, the citizens appreciate the state's beauty and freedoms. As Montana writer Joseph Kinsey Howard puts it, "Where is there more opportunity to enjoy the elemental values of living, bright sun and clean air and space? We have room. We can be neighbors without getting in each other's hair. We can be individuals." Montana's population may be sparse, but its people are diverse and its heritage rich.

Picking flowers near Bannack

Population

Montana's population has grown and declined several times during its history. It reached its officially recorded peak of 826,000 in 1985. According to the 1990 census, Montana has 803,655 residents and ranks as the forty-fourth state in population.

Just more than half of Montana's citizens live in urban areas. Only nine cities have a population of more than 10,000. Most of

Opposite: A young Montanan in Bull River Valley

Native Americans were Montana's first residents.

these are in the western third of the state. Billings and Great Falls are the only two cities with more than 55,000 people. The 1990 census reported 81,151 residents in Billings and 55,097 residents in Great Falls.

The First Residents

Montana's first residents were American Indians. The influx of white settlers from the 1860s to the early 1900s and the federal government's policy of restricting Native Americans to reservations overwhelmed the native tribes. Today, Native Americans are the state's only large racial minority.

Members of eleven tribes—almost 50,000 individuals—live in Montana, accounting for just less than 6 percent of the population.

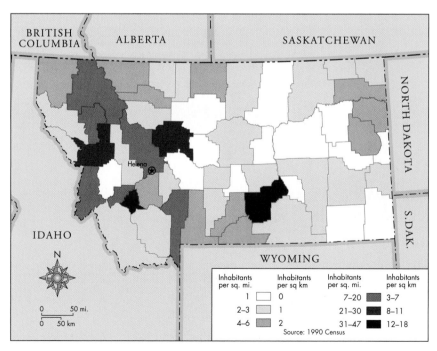

Montana's population density

Firsts for Native American Women

Susan "Walking Bear" Yellowtail, born in 1903, attended a seminary in Massachusetts, then completed her nurse's training at Boston General Hospital. A member of the Crow tribe in Pryor, she became the first Native American registered nurse in the United States.

Born in 1901, Dolly Smith Cusker Akers grew up in Wolf Point. In 1932, she became the first Native American elected to the Montana state legislature. In 1964, Akers served as area vice president of the National Congress of American Indians. She died in 1986. ▩

Nearly two-thirds reside on seven federally controlled reservations. Most of the others live in Billings, Missoula, and Great Falls.

The Native American population of Montana has more than quadrupled since 1900, showing an increase of 27.9 percent from 1980 to 1990. Montana ranks fifth among the states for the number of Native Americans in its population.

Other Ethnic Groups

After the Lewis and Clark expedition opened the area, people from various ethnic groups found their way to Montana. Gold seekers from Ireland, England, Germany, and the Scandinavian countries followed French-Canadian and British fur traders. Chinese immigrants came to work the mines and labor in mining camps. After the Civil War, some African-Americans arrived, but state laws restricting the activities of Asians and African-Americans forced many to leave.

Copper mining brought immigrants from Ireland, Wales, England, Italy, Poland, Greece, Austria, Finland, and Yugoslavia. Many

Population of Montana's Major Cities (1990)

City	Population
Billings	81,151
Great Falls	55,097
Missoula	42,918
Butte	33,941
Helena	24,569
Bozeman	22,600

Hutterites

Related to the Amish and the Mennonites, Montana's Hutterites (above) live in some forty colonies in the central part of the state. These three religious groups originated in sixteenth-century Europe during the Protestant Reformation. The Hutterites first arrived in Montana in 1911. They are known for their strong traditions, work ethic, pacifism, thrift, and skills in agriculture. ■

settled in Butte, Anaconda, and Great Falls. During the height of the mining era, as many as thirty languages might have been heard on the streets of Montana's mining towns.

In the early 1900s, tens of thousands of immigrants, mostly from Germany and the Scandinavian countries, were lured to the high plains by advertisements that made incredible promises about the land along Montana's northern tier—the Hi-Line. More recent arrivals include Mexican laborers brought north in the 1940s to harvest sugar beets and Southeast Asians who came to the Missoula area in the 1970s.

Some of Montana's immigrant groups have remained close-knit. Hollanders settled in the Gallatin Valley in 1890 and still retain many Dutch traditions. A group of Finns give the lumbering community of Milltown the flavor of Finland. The Hutterites, a religious group similar to Canada's Mennonites and the Amish of Pennsylvania, live in prosperous but tightly knit communes.

According to the 1990 census, 92.75 percent of Montanans identified themselves as white, 5.97 percent as Native American, 1.52 percent as Hispanic, 0.53 percent as Asian or Pacific Islander, and 0.30 percent as African-American. About 0.45 percent were of other races.

Education

The first schools in Montana were established in mining camps—in Bannack and Nevada City in 1863 and in Virginia City in 1866. Roman Catholic schools at St. Mary's Mission (later Fort Owen) and St. Ignatius's Mission also offered classes. In 1865, Montana's first legislative assembly ordered that a territorial public school system established. School attendance for children between eight and sixteen was made a requirement in 1883.

Four years after statehood, Montana created a state board of education. High schools, first opened privately in the state in 1881, became part of the free public school system in 1897.

Montana's impressive school system is due to voter support and the 1972 constitution, which stressed the importance of education. Only seven states have higher percentages of teens completing high school. The state's adult literacy rate is well above the national average. The state's school system includes public and private elementary and high schools, state universities, technical colleges, private and tribal colleges, and community colleges.

The University of Montana in Missoula

Colleges and Universities

The state's first college, founded in Deer Lodge in 1878, was called Montana Collegiate Institute. In 1893, Montana created its state university system. The University of Montana at Missoula and Montana State University at Bozeman were chartered that year.

The Montana university system has six units. Montana State University is the largest, with a 1997 enrollment of more than 10,000. The University of Montana comes second, with 9,806 students. Other universities in the system include Montana State-Billings (formerly Eastern Montana College), Montana Tech of the University of Montana (formerly Montana College of Mineral Sciences and Technology) in Butte, Montana State-Northern (formerly Northern Montana College) in Havre, and Western Montana College in Dillon.

The Roman Catholic Church operates Carroll College in Helena and the University of Great Falls. Other private colleges include Rocky Mountain College, sponsored by the Congregational, Methodist, and Presbyterian Churches, Montana Bible College, Yellowstone Bible College, and Mountain States Baptist College.

Montana is the only state with a tribally controlled college on each of its reservations: Blackfeet Community College, Dull Knife Memorial College, Fort Belknap College, Fort Peck Community College, Salish-Kootenai College, Little Bighorn Community

Cathedral of St. Helena

This house of worship, built from 1908 to 1924, is modeled after the Cologne Cathedral in Germany and the Votive Cathedral of the Sacred Heart in Austria.

The church has stained-glass windows from Germany that depict the seven holy sacraments and a white marble altar from Italy. Dominating the capital's skyline with its twin 230-foot (70-m) spires, the Cathedral of St. Helena lends an air of European dignity to the western city. ■

College, and Stone Child College. Three other community colleges, in Glendive, Kalispell, and Miles City, offer classes.

Religion

Almost half of Montana's citizens belong to an organized religious group. Most are Protestant, but the largest single group is Roman Catholic. In 1990, the state had some 200 Catholic churches. The Evangelical Lutheran Church and the Church of Jesus Christ of Latter-day Saints, or Mormons, also have important presences in Montana.

CHAPTER TEN

Inspiration and Excellence

Montanans enjoy a vast array of recreational activities centered on arts and sports. They are accustomed to driving hundreds of miles to attend a high school football game, visit an arts festival, or take part in some of the nation's best hunting, fishing, skiing, hiking, and camping.

Montana is home to a number of writers, artists, and performers. Specialties as diverse as quilting, cowboy poetry, fiddling, and chainsaw sculpture find audiences throughout the state. Montanans support numerous folk-arts organizations, festivals, fairs, and Native American powwows. Art shows, auctions, public museums, and galleries can be found in dozens of Montana cities.

Montana's finest museums reflect geology, history, industry, ethnic heritage, and the art of the state. Historical museums include the Montana Historical Society Museum in Helena and museums at Big Hole National Battlefield in Wisdom and Little Bighorn Battlefield National Monument. Geology and prehistory exhibits are presented at the Museum of the Rocky Mountains in Bozeman. The World Museum of Mining is in Butte. The Museum of the Plains Indian and Craft Center in Browning has an extensive collection of historic and contemporary art and artifacts.

Cross-country skiing is just one of Montana's outdoor activities.

Opposite: Hiking in Glacier National Park

Inside the Museum of the Plains Indian and Craft Center

Writers

The Last Best Place is an anthology of works by Montana writers who captured the essence of their state in story, song, poetry, history, and fiction. The tradition began with the diaries of Montana's earliest settlers and the stories and songs of its Native Americans. Authors such as Teddy Blue Abbot, Andrew Garcia, and Frank Bird Linderman recorded the early history of the state.

In 1919, H. G. Merriam founded a creative-writing program at the University of Montana at Missoula. His literary journal, *Frontier and Midland,* published student writings from authors such as A. B. Guthrie Jr. and Dorothy Johnson.

Alfred Bertram Guthrie Jr. (1901–1991) grew up in Choteau and Great Falls. A graduate of the University of Montana, he taught writing and worked as a journalist and editor in Kentucky before writing the novels about Montana that made him famous. His stories, written from his home in Choteau, told of the people who made Montana great. *The Big Sky, These Thousand Hills,* and *The Last Valley* are still read. *The Way West* won the Pulitzer Prize in 1950.

Raised in Whitefish, Dorothy Johnson (1905–1984) wrote Western stories that inspired several movies. Her works included *The Man Who Shot Liberty Valance, The Hanging Tree,* and *A Man Called Horse.* Johnson spent fifteen years as a book and magazine editor in New York before coming home to Montana to edit the *Whitefish Pilot* and teach journalism.

Richard Hugo, a respected poet who greatly influenced regional literature, became director of H. G. Merriam's creative-writing program at the University of Montana at Missoula in 1964. Through the years, many well-known writers have been associated with the program, including William Kittredge and James Crumley.

Norman Maclean, who grew up in Missoula, didn't begin to write about Montana until later in life. One of his novels, *A River Runs Through It,* was made into a major motion picture.

Another renowned author, Joseph Kinsey Howard, wrote one of the most respected histories of the state in 1943. Howard, who graduated from high school in Great Falls in 1923, gained fame as a journalist, regional historian, and social and political critic. His book, *Montana: High, Wide, and Handsome* is considered a definitive look at the social, economic, and political history of Montana, even though his views were controversial. A. B. Guthrie called him "Montana's conscience . . . the greatest Montanan of our time, perhaps of any time." Howard died in 1951.

A. B. Guthrie Jr. won the Pulitzer Prize for *The Way West*.

Dorothy Johnson wrote many Western novels.

Norman Maclean (1902–1990)

Raised in Missoula, Norman Maclean (right) spent much of his life as an English professor at the University of Chicago and didn't begin writing about Montana until he was seventy years old. *A River Runs Through It and Other Stories* (1976), detailing his youth, centers on his many happy hours of fly-fishing in the Blackfoot River. ■

Charles M. Russell

Artists and Cartoonists

Of the hundreds of regional artists and artisans in Montana, the best known is cowboy artist Charles "Charlie" M. Russell (1864–1926). As an author, a painter, and bronze sculptor, Russell depicted homesteaders' lives on the open range with exceptional insight and sensitivity.

Russell came to Montana in 1880 at the age of sixteen. A rebellious youth from a wealthy St. Louis family, Charlie was sent west by his father in an attempt to discipline the young man. A mountain man named Jake Hoover took Charlie in and taught him how to survive in the western wilderness. Later, while working as a night wrangler for a cattle ranch, Charlie spent his days painting, drawing, and sculpting. After ten years in the saddle, he knew firsthand about the hardships of the open range. He incorporated this knowledge into his paintings and sculptures.

Russell's body of work includes more than 4,500 oil paintings, watercolors, sculptures, and illustrated letters. He is the only artist honored in Statuary Hall in the U.S. Capitol.

Another Montana artist, Terri Mimnaugh, created the Jeannette Rankin statue that stands in Washington, D.C. The statue commemorates Rankin's contributions to the U.S. Congress during her years as a Montana representative.

John L. Clarke (1881–1970)

Born in Highwood, John L. Clarke (right) became deaf as a toddler after suffering from scarlet fever. A noted sculptor, painter, and carver, he became nationally known for his landscapes of the Glacier National Park region. He was known as *Cutapuis* (Man-Who-Talks-Not) to the Blackfeet. His large-scale murals of Blackfeet life are displayed at the Museum of the Plains Indian in Browning and at the School for the Deaf and Blind in Great Falls. ■

Stan Lynde, creator of the *Rick O'Shay* comic strip, entertained 20 million readers in 100 newspapers nationwide via the *Chicago Tribune–New York News* wire service from 1958 until 1977. His other strip, *Latigo,* ran in the same newspapers from 1979 until the mid-1980s.

Another artist familiar to practically everyone in Montana is Monte Dolack. He creates watercolor and acrylic animal posters and prints and handmade lithographs. Born in Great Falls, Dolack worked for the Anaconda Copper Company and played in local rock bands before turning to art. Dolack's humor comes through in his works, some of which have become valuable and collectible. Dolack owns an art gallery in Missoula.

TV journalist Chet Huntley

Television and Movies

Montana's best-known contribution to television was Chet Huntley of the *Huntley–Brinkley Report* on NBC News. Chester Robert Huntley was born in Cardwell in 1911. He retired from the network after more than thirty years of television journalism but continued to broadcast weekly radio commentaries until his death in 1974.

**Gary Cooper in
*High Noon***

More than seventy feature films, television productions, and scenes were filmed in Montana during the twentieth century. Some of these include *Little Big Man, The Shining, The Untouchables, Always, A River Runs Through It, Far and Away, Forrest Gump, Return to Lonesome Dove, Under Siege II: Dark Territory,* and *The Horse Whisperer.*

Movie stars Gary Cooper and Myrna Loy came from Montana. Frank James Cooper (1901–1961) was born in Helena. As Gary Cooper, his career began in silent films in the 1920s. By 1937, he was earning more than any other movie star. Cooper appeared in more than ninety movies. His performances in *Sergeant York* (1941) and *High Noon* (1952) earned him Academy Awards as best actor.

Myrna Adele Williams (1905–1993) was better known to the movie going public as Myrna Loy. Born in Radersburg, Myrna Loy began her career as a chorus girl in 1925, moving to the big screen the next year. Known as the Queen of the Movies, she starred as Nora Charles in *The Thin Man*. The Myrna Loy Center for the Performing Arts in Helena chronicles her many films.

A Love of Sports

Montanans love sports of all kinds, from football, baseball, and basketball to volleyball, tennis, golf, and track and field. Sailing, hockey, bowling, equestrian events, swimming, skiing, and biking also draw spectators and participants.

The rivalry between the Montana State University Bobcats and the University of Montana Grizzlies began in 1897—and shows no signs of flagging after more than a century. Fans travel from all over the state to witness the annual battles between these two teams.

Baseball

Baseball has been a popular pastime in Montana since the 1860s, when games were played in the mining camps. Today, several minor-league teams, such as the Helena Brewers, the Great Falls Dodgers, the Butte Copper Kings, and the Billings Mustangs, play in the Pioneer League. These teams are farm clubs for major-league teams in the National and American Leagues.

Several major-league stars have played for Montana teams. George Brett, 1976 and 1980 American League batting champion, played for Billings. George Bell, who played for Helena in 1978, played for the Toronto Blue Jays when he was chosen the American League's Most Valuable Player in 1987. Dave McNally began his pitching career in Billings, before going on to play for the Baltimore Orioles.

Olympians

Almost a dozen athletes from Montana have participated in the Olympics. Gene Davis, from Missoula County High School, won a bronze medal in Montreal in 1976 for freestyle wrestling and coached the U.S. team in Seoul, South Korea, in 1988.

Lones Wigger Jr. of Carter has won more Olympic medals than any other Montana athlete, taking home the gold medal in 1964 in Tokyo for the three-position small-bore shooting event and the silver medal in the prone small-bore event that same year. In 1972, in Munich, Germany, he captured the gold medal in the three-position free-rifle event. Wigger has won more than eighty national championships and holds twenty-nine world records and thirty-two U.S. records.

Dave McNally (1942–)

Baseball aficionados are proud of Montana native Dave McNally. In the 1970 World Series, McNally pitched for the Baltimore Orioles and hit a grand slam home run in the third game, helping defeat the Cincinnati Red Sox. The Orioles went on to win the series. McNally, now retired from baseball, lives in Billings. ■

High Altitude Sports Center

Butte is home to the highest sports center in the world. The High Altitude Sports Center, at 5,528 feet (1,686 m), provides an opportunity for athletes to train in demanding conditions that would make most athletes gasp for breath. The center's speed-skating oval is the national training site for the U.S. speed-skating team. ■

Rodeo

Considered by some to be the world's roughest sport, rodeo always draws huge audiences in Montana. Bronc riding, steer roping and wrestling, and bull riding separate "fence-post" cowboys from true cowboys. Dozens of rodeos are staged each summer in Montana, offering chances for cowboys and cowgirls of all ages to participate in fun and prizes.

Alice Greenough Orr (1902–1995)

One of Montana's most famous cowboys is a cowgirl! Alice Greenough Orr (left) was born in Red Lodge and earned the title Queen of the Bronc Riders. Orr won four world saddle bronc championships in the 1930s and 1940s. In 1975, she was the first person inducted into the Cowgirl Hall of Fame. In 1983, she added induction into the National Cowboy Hall of Fame to her long list of accomplishments. ■

The Iditarod

For twenty-three years, Alaskans won every one of the 1,049-mile (1,688-km) Iditarod Trail Sled Dog Races between Anchorage and Nome, Alaska. In 1995, however, the winner hailed from the town of Simms, Montana. Doug Swingley gained the lead early in the grueling race and never looked back.

Doug Swingley, winner of the 1995 Iditarod

Fishing and Hunting

Fishing in Montana is a year-round sport. There are 4 million acres (1.6 million ha) of cold-water lakes in the state; 15,000 miles (24,135 km) of cold-water streams; 6,100 miles (9,815 km) of warm-water rivers and streams; and 350,000 acres (141,750 ha) of warm-water lakes. Some 28 percent of all Montanans purchase a license every year to fish for rainbow trout, kokanee salmon, walleye, and large-mouth bass.

Montana hunters take deer, elk, moose, antelope, bighorn sheep, mountain goats, and black bears. Hunters seeking trophies know they will find what they are looking for in Montana's beautiful forests, lakes, streams, and mountains.

Fly-fishing on Bett Cree

Timeline

United States History

1607 The first permanent English settlement is established in North America at Jamestown.

1620 Pilgrims found Plymouth Colony, the second permanent English settlement.

1776 America declares its independence from Britain.

1783 The Treaty of Paris officially ends the Revolutionary War in America.

1787 The U.S. Constitution is written.

1803 The Louisiana Purchase almost doubles the size of the United States.

1812–15 The United States and Britain fight the War of 1812.

1861–65 The North and South fight each other in the American Civil War.

Montana State History

1762 France surrenders Montana to Spain.

1800 France reclaims Montana.

1803 Eastern Montana becomes part of the United States with the Louisiana Purchase.

1805 The Lewis and Clark Expedition reaches Montana.

1841 Father Pierre Jean de Smet founds St. Mary's Mission in Bitterroot Valley.

1862 Gold is discovered on Grasshopper Creek.

1864 The Montana Territory is created by the U.S. Congress.

1866 The great cattle drives to Montana begin.

United States History

The United States is **1917–18** involved in World War I.

The stock market crashes, **1929** plunging the United States into the Great Depression.

The United States **1941–45** fights in World War II.
The United States becomes a **1945** charter member of the U.N.

The United States **1951–53** fights in the Korean War.

The U.S. Congress enacts a series of **1964** groundbreaking civil rights laws.

The United States **1964–73** engages in the Vietnam War.

The United States and other **1991** nations fight the brief Persian Gulf War against Iraq.

Montana State History

1876 The Dakota and the Cheyenne defeat General Custer's troops in the Battle of Little Bighorn.

1889 Montana becomes the forty-first state on November 8.

1910 Congress creates Glacier National Park.

1940 Fort Peck Dam is completed.

1973 A new state constitution takes effect.

1996 Unabomber Theodore Kaczynski is captured.

Fast Facts

State capitol

Statehood date	November 8, 1889, the 41st state
Origin of state name	Spanish for "mountainous"
State capital	Helena
State nickname	Treasure State; Big Sky Country
State motto	*Oro y Plata* (Gold and Silver)
State bird	Western meadowlark
State flower	Bitterroot
State mammal	Grizzly bear
State fish	Blackspotted cutthroat trout
State fossil	Duck-billed dinosaur
State grass	Bluebunch wheatgrass
State tree	Ponderosa pine
State gemstones	Sapphire and moss agate
State song	"Montana"
State fair	Great Falls (late July–early August)
Total area; rank	147,046 sq. mi. (380,849 sq km); 4th

The Absaroka
Mountain Range

Land; rank	145,556 sq. mi. (376,990 sq km); 4th
Water; rank	1,490 sq. mi. (3,859 sq km); 19th
Inland water; rank	1,490 sq. mi. (3,859 sq km); 15th
Geographic center	8 miles (13 km) west of Lewistown
Latitude and longitude	Montana is located approximately between 44° 23' and 49° N and 104° 02' and 116° 03' W
Highest point	Granite Peak, 12,799 feet (3,904 m)
Lowest point	1,800 feet (549 m) above sea level along the Kootenai River in Lincoln County
Largest city	Billings
Number of counties	56
Population; rank	803,655 (1990 census); 44th
Density	5 persons per sq. mi. (2 per sq km)
Population distribution	52% urban, 48% rural

Ethnic distribution (does not equal 100%)

White	92.75%
Native American	5.97%
Hispanic	1.52%
Asian and Pacific Islanders	0.53%
Other	0.45%
African-American	0.30%

Flower field in Bannack

Record high temperature	117°F (47°C) at Glendive on July 20, 1893, and at Medicine Lake on July 5, 1937
Record low temperature	–70°F (–57°C) at Rogers Pass on on January 20, 1954
Average July temperature	68°F (20°C)

Average January temperature 18°F (–8°C)

Average annual precipitation 15 inches (38 cm)

Big Hole National Battlefield

Natural Areas and Historic Sites

National Battlefield
Big Hole National Battlefield preserves the site of the 1877 conflict between the U.S. Army and the Nez Perce.

National Recreation Area
Bighorn Canyon National Recreation Area contains Bighorn Lake, formed by the building of the Yellowtail Dam on the Bighorn River in 1966. Parts of the recreation area are in Wyoming.

National Historic Sites
Fort Union Trading Post National Historic Site was the site of a major fur-trading post on the Upper Missouri River from 1829 to 1867. Parts of the site are in North Dakota

Grant-Kohrs Ranch National Historic Site was the headquarters of one of the largest nineteenth-century range ranches in the United States.

National Parks
Glacier National Park preserves dramatic glaciers, lakes, and mountains and abundant wildflowers and wildlife.

Yellowstone National Park, the first national park in the United States, contains one of the finest geyser fields in the world. Parts of the park are in Wyoming and Idaho.

National Historical Park
Nez Perce National Historical Park commemorates the history and culture of the Nez Perce. Parts of the park are in Washington, Idaho, and Oregon.

Glacier National Park

Giant Springs State Park

National Monument

Little Bighorn Battlefield National Monument is the site of the Battle of Little Bighorn in which troops of General George Custer were defeated by the combined forces of the Dakota and Northern Cheyenne.

State Parks

Montana maintains more than forty state parks. *Flathead Lake State Park, West Shore State Park,* and *Yellow Bay State Park* all circle Flathead Lake, one of the largest lakes in the West. Montana's badlands can be enjoyed in both *Makoshika State Park* and *Medicine Rocks State Park.*

Sports Teams

NCAA Teams (Division 1)

Montana State University Bobcats

University of Montana Grizzlies

Cultural Institutions

Libraries

Library of the State Historical Society in Helena contains the world's largest collection on the history of the Montana area.

Montana State University Library in Billings contains significant collections on General Custer and the Battle of Little Bighorn.

Museums

The Museum of the Rockies in Bozeman features exhibits on Rocky Mountain geology, archaeology, and fossils.

The Museum of the Plains Indian and Craft Center in Browning houses historical and contemporary American Indian art collections.

The World Museum of Mining in Butte highlights the history of mining and the evolution of mining techniques.

Museum of the Plains Indian and Craft Center

University of Montana

Winter in Montana

The Montana Historical Society houses the state's historical collections and the art of Western artist Charles M. Russell.

Performing Arts
All Montana's larger cities have community symphony orchestras and centers for the performing arts. Many cities also have community and university drama and dance groups.

Universities and Colleges
In the mid-1990s, Montana had nineteen public and nine private institutions of higher learning.

Annual Events

January–March
National Outdoor Speedskating Championship in Butte (January)

"Race to the Sky" Sled Dog Race, Helena to Seeley Lake (February)

Winter Carnival in Whitefish (February)

Winter Carnival in Red Lodge (March)

April–June
Cherry Blossom Festival in Polson (May)

College National Finals Rodeo in Bozeman (June)

Great Falls Railroad Show in Great Falls (June)

Governor's Cup Marathon in Helena (June)

Music Festival in Red Lodge (June)

Montana Traditional Jazz Festival in Helena (June)

Walleye Fishing Tournament in Havre (June)

July–September
Home of Champions Rodeo in Red Lodge (July)

Libby Logger Days in Libby (July)

Livingston Roundup in Livingston (July)

State Fiddler's Contest in Polson (July)

Yellowstone River Valley

North American Indian Days in Browning (July)

Wild Horse Stampede Rodeo in Wolf Point (July)

Yellowstone River Float, Livingston to Billings (July)

Festival of Nations in Red Lodge (August)

Northwest Montana Fair and Rodeo in Kalispell (August)

Sweet Pea Art Festival in Bozeman (August)

Western Montana Fair and Rodeo in Missoula (August)

Threshing Bee and Antique Show in Culbertson (September)

October–December

Bison Roundup near Moiese (October)

Northern International Stock Show and Rodeo in Billings (October)

Bald Eagle Gathering near Helena (November)

Fall Camp for Cross-Country Skiers in West Yellowstone (November)

Christmas Stroll in Bozeman (December)

Famous People

Gary Cooper

Gary Cooper (1901–1961)	Actor
A. B. Guthrie Jr. (1901–1991)	Writer
James J. Hill (1838–1916)	Railroad entrepreneur
Chet Huntley (1911–1974)	Journalist and commentator
Dorothy M. Johnson (1905–1984)	Writer
Myrna Loy (1905–1993)	Actress
David Lynch (1946–)	Filmmaker
Norman Maclean (1902–1990)	Writer
Dave McNally (1942–)	Baseball player
Alice Greenough Orr (1902–1995)	Saddle bronc rider
Plenty Coups (1848–1932)	Crow chief
Jeannette Rankin (1880–1973)	Suffragist and public official
Charles M. Russell (1864–1926)	Artist
Sacajawea (1786?–1812?)	Indian guide
Washakie (1804?–1900)	Shoshone chief

To Find Out More

History

- Fradin, Dennis Brindell. *Montana*. Chicago: Childrens Press, 1992.

- LaDoux, Rita. *Montana*. Minneapolis: Lerner, 1992.

- Patent, Dorothy Hinshaw. *Where the Bald Eagles Gather*. New York: Clarion Books, 1990.

- Shirley, Gayle C. *Montana Wildlife: A Children's Field Guide to the State's Most Remarkable Animals*. Helena: Falcon Publishing Company, 1996.

- Thompson, Kathleen. *Montana*. Austin, Tex.: Raintree/Steck-Vaughn, 1996.

Biography

- Blumberg, Rhoda. *The Incredible Journey of Lewis & Clark*. Surrey, England: Beech Tree Books, 1995.

- Faber, Doris. *Calamity Jane: Her Life and Her Legend*. New York: Houghton Mifflin, 1992.

- St. George, Judith. *Sacagawea*. New York: Philomel Books, 1997.

Fiction

- Corcoran, Barbara. *Wolf at the Door*. New York: Atheneum, 1993.

- Stewart, Jennifer. *If That Breathes Fire, We're Toast!* New York: Holiday House, 1999.

- Van Steenwyk, Elizabeth. *Three Dog Winter*. New York: Yearling Books, 1999.

Websites

- **Montana Historical Society**
  http://www.his.state.mt.us/
  Offers a cybertour of its historical collections and links to other resources

- **Montana Online**
  http://www.state.mt.us/
  The official website for the state of Montana

Addresses

- **Montana Legislative Council**
  Room 138
  State Capitol
  Helena, MT 59620
  For information on Montana's government

- **Montana Historical Society**
  225 N. Roberts Street
  Helena, MT 59620
  For information on Montana's history

- **Department of Commerce**
  Census and Economic Information Center
  1424 9th Avenue
  Helena, MT 59620
  For information on Montana's economy

- **Department of Commerce**
  Montana Promotion Division
  1424 9th Avenue
  Helena, MT 59620
  For information about tourism in Montana

Index

Page numbers in *italics* indicate illustrations.

Meet the Authors

Charles George received a bachelor's degree in Spanish and history from Tarleton State University in Stephenville, Texas. He taught Spanish and social studies for fifteen years on the high school level, then retired to write full-time. He became an instructor with the Institute of Children's Literature in February 2000.

Linda George received a bachelor's degree in elementary education from the University of Texas at El Paso. She taught at the elementary school level for ten years. In 1979, she began her professional writing career. She has been an instructor at the Institute of Children's Literature since 1998.

"The highlight of our visit to Montana," the Georges say, "had to be crossing Beartooth Pass one foggy day, pulling our travel trailer. Even in the mist, the view was captivating. At the top of the pass, we scrambled for sweaters and coats, enduring icy winds to stand in awe of our incredible surroundings."

Photo Credits